KINDLY
LIGHT

KINDLY LIGHT

THE STORY OF
BLIND VETERANS UK

ANDREW NORMAN

FONTHILL

To my beloved late grandfather, St Dunstaner Thomas Waldin,
formerly of the 8th Rifle Brigade.

Fonthill Media Language Policy

Fonthill Media publishes in the international English language market. One language edition is published worldwide. As there are minor differences in spelling and presentation, especially with regard to American English and British English, a policy is necessary to define which form of English to use. The Fonthill Policy is to use the form of English native to the author. Andrew Norman was born and educated in England and now lives at Poole in Dorset, therefore British English has been adopted in this publication.

Fonthill Media Limited
Fonthill Media LLC
www.fonthillmedia.com
office@fonthillmedia.com

First published in the United Kingdom
and the United States of America 2015

British Library Cataloguing in Publication Data:
A catalogue record for this book is available from the British Library

ISBN 978-1-78155-389-3

Typeset in 10pt on 13pt Minion Pro
Printed and bound in England

Contents

Blind Veterans UK

Blind Veterans UK is a national charity that offers support, rehabilitation, and training, together with residential and respite care where necessary, to former men and women of the Armed Services who suffer from a loss of vision.

They believe that no one should be obliged to battle blindness alone. That is why they provide ex-Service men and women with free services and lifelong practical and emotional support, regardless of when they served or how they lost their sight. Their aim is to help such blind veterans to recover their independence and discover life beyond sight loss.

Blind Veterans UK operates from three centres: Brighton and Sheffield in England, and Llandudno in Wales, with welfare officers available to visit members in their homes.

The organization relies on donations, and on numerous volunteers who offer help with a wide range of activities.

For further information, please visit www.blindveterans.org.uk.

In 1915 my Great-Grandfather Sir Arthur Pearson founded St Dunstan's an organization which provided exemplary care and training for the war-blinded Allied servicemen of the First World War. As a family we feel thrilled to have his portrait in our home. Whenever I feel times are difficult I just look at his wise face with it's sightless eyes and think that if he could manage blind I must succeed with normal eye sight.
St Dunstan's continues to-day as 'Blind Veterans UK' and its standards of excellence have been maintained, admired and copied Worldwide.

Marina Egerton-Warburton

Author's Note

It is impossible in a single volume, to pay adequate tribute to the thousands of St Dunstaners (both men and women) and to the doctors, nurses, VADs, volunteers, and families who worked with them with love and dedication to turn their lives around.

Therefore, inevitably, the focus is on Sir Arthur Pearson; his background, and the circumstances which led him to found this great enterprise (now known as 'Blind Veterans UK').

This account begins with Pearson's early life. As he matured from boyhood to manhood, those characteristics which would one day stand him in good stead as 'Father' of the blind servicemen of the First World War, would become more and more evident: determination, courage, curiosity, flair, leadership, but most important of all, compassion.

Acknowledgements

I am grateful to the following museums, colleges, groups, and institutions: Blind Foundation, New Zealand; British Medical Association; Canadian National Institute for the Blind; Eton College; Helen Keller International; Imperial War Museum; IPC London; Islington and Camden Cemetery Services; Library and Archives, Canada; Moorfields Eye Hospital and Institute of Ophthalmology; National Army Museum; National Federation of the Blind, USA; Pearson's Holiday Fund; Poole Central Library; Royal College of Anaesthetists; Royal College of Ophthalmologists; Royal College of Physicians of England; Royal College of Surgeons of England; Royal Green Jackets' Museum, Winchester; The Scout Association; South African National Council for the Blind; Veterans Affairs, Canada; Vision Australia; and Winchester College Archives.

The following individuals were extremely generous in their help and support: Peter Adams; John B. Atkins; Alan Baker; Margaret Berryman; D. J. Bignell; Doreen Birks; Ian Causland; Sara Chatfield; Eileen Crewes; Patricia Dean; Gabriel Dragffy; Joanna Ellis; David Gibson; Ken Gray; Judith Haswell; Penny Hatfield; Alison Jones; Richard Keeler; Jean Kelly; Barry King; Louise King; Michael Gordon-Lennox; Liz Martin; Alastair Massie; The Dowager Marchioness of Normanby; The Marquis of Normanby; Don Planner; Mark Quinlan; Bryan K. H. Rogers; Mathieu Sabourin; James Sanders; Theo V. Thomas; and Diana and Alan Turner.

I'm also grateful to my family, particularly Jean Norman, Jane Savery, and Peter, David, and Howard Waldin for their kindness in loaning photographs, and for sharing their memories with me.

I am deeply grateful to both Robert Baker, Information and Archives Officer, Blind Veterans UK (formerly St Dunstan's), and to Richard Keeler, for their unstinting assistance to me.

I am especially grateful to Sir Arthur Pearson's granddaughter Sally Hardy, and to his great-granddaughter Marya Egerton-Warburton.

And lastly I am deeply grateful to my beloved wife Rachel for all her help and encouragement.

Lead, kindly Light, amid the encircling gloom,
Lead Thou me on;
The night is dark, and I am far from home,
Lead Thou me on.
Keep Thou my feet; I do not ask to see
The distant scene; one step enough for me.

Reverend John Henry Newman (1801–90)

Preface

The year is 1915; the place, a workshop in the grounds of a London mansion. From this workshop emanates the deafening sound of men hammering nails into hobnail boots. Competing with this cacophony is the sound of their voices, singing old favourites like 'It's a Long Way to Tipperary' and 'There's a Long, Long Trail a Winding'—songs which, not long ago, they sang with other comrades in France and Belgium. The 'Cobblers' Chorus' reflects the sense of purpose and satisfaction in what they are doing, when only a short time ago, their lives seemed futile and empty. These men are not only from Britain but also from around the Commonwealth—Australia, New Zealand, Canada, Rhodesia, and South Africa. They have been shelled, bombed, mined, shot at, and gassed on the insatiable killing fields of the Western Front and on other fronts, and have emerged bleeding, broken and—all of them—sightless.

An observer, having overcome his or her initial astonishment, would wonder a), how, given their circumstances, these men could seem so happy, and b), how they could possibly do the job that they were doing, and just as well as any sighted person, if not better?

The workshop was situated at St Dunstan's in London, and Arthur (later 'Sir Arthur') Pearson was the man responsible for this seemingly miraculous transformation in the lives of the 'St Dunstaners'. The primary focus of this book is Sir Arthur Pearson—the man, his background, the circumstances that led him to found this great enterprise of St Dunstan's (now known as 'Blind Veterans UK'), and how this former newspaper proprietor, who had no medical or psychological knowledge or training, managed to achieve such success in establishing a charitable foundation.

As for the St Dunstaners, it is impossible in a single volume to pay adequate tribute to them, or to the myriad of doctors, nurses, VADs, volunteers, families, and friends who accompanied them on their journey from despair to, in Pearson's phrase, 'Victory Over Blindness'. However, by recounting some of their experiences, some insight may be gained into the challenges that they faced, and how St Dunstan's, founded over a century ago, evolved and adapted to suit their varying needs.

Here are to be found true and heart-warming stories of great courage, comradeship, and dedication on the part of Pearson and his staff, and of the astonishing feats achieved by those who proved that to be blind does not necessarily preclude gainful employment, romance, love, marriage, and a happy family life.

St Dunstan's, beneath the great clock. (*Blind Veterans UK*)

Arthur Pearson: Early Life

(Cyril) Arthur Pearson was born on 24 February 1866 at Wookey in Somerset, where his father, the Reverend (Arthur) Cyril Pearson, was curate at the Church of St Matthew. His mother was Philippa Massingberd Pearson (née Maxwell-Lyte) whose grandfather, the Reverend Henry Francis Lyte, wrote the words to one of the most moving hymns in the English language—'Abide with Me'. Pearson had four younger sisters: Ethel (b. 1867), Mabel (b. 1868), Marion (b. 1869), and Olive (b. 1871).[1]

From 1876, Pearson attended Eagle House Preparatory School in Wimbledon, where on the cricket pitch he showed potential as a promising bowler. In 1877 his father became Rector of Drayton Parslow in Buckinghamshire. In January 1880, following in his father's footsteps, Pearson became a pupil at Winchester College[2] in Hampshire, starting as a Commoner in 'D' House. Given the nickname 'Pigeon', he proved to be both popular and sociable. Pearson was 'always up to some merry prank or other, and was famous for telling the funniest stories night after night'. He (and his father) were 'wonderful hands at riddles, puzzles, chess problems, acrostics, and tricks of all kinds.'[3] In fact, the Reverend Pearson would go on to have books published on such subjects, including *One Hundred Chess Problems* (1878), *The Twentieth Century Standard Puzzle Book*, and *The Twentieth Century Standard Problem Book* (both 1907); the latter was devoted to the solving of mathematical problems—or 'recreational mathematics'. Not to be outdone, his wife Philippa wrote *The Acrostic Dictionary*, which was published in 1901.

At the end of his first term, Pearson was awarded prize money—for the purchase of books—after coming top of his class. He also threw himself enthusiastically into sport, playing cricket for his house (his father before him had played for the school's 1st XI), and won a reputation for being 'a most tricky bowler amongst the Juniors'.[4] On the annual athletics day in 1881, he competed in an event listed as the 'Wide [long] Jump—For all under 5ft 4in [tall] and 16 years [of age]'.

> This event was easily won by Pearson, with an extremely fine jump, which he accomplished after several attempts, in the greater number of which he fell backwards and lost his jump. Grant and Hardy were the next best, but considerably behind Pearson.

In the following year, 1882, he competed in the hurdles, 100 yards and 200 yards flat races, as well as wide jump (again).[5] Pearson also enjoyed hockey and lawn tennis. In fact, outwardly, all appeared to be well with him, both at work and play. However, in reality this was far from the case, for as Gerald Fiennes, one of his contemporaries, candidly said, 'He was too blind to play games well'.[6] The truth was that Pearson's eyesight was already beginning to fail, and this would have profound implications for his future. In the meantime, this did not prevent Pearson from sending off articles which he had composed to a weekly magazine called *Tit-Bits*, founded by Sir George Newnes in Manchester in 1881.

Pearson's time at Winchester College was cut short, not because of his poor sight, but because his father could no longer afford to pay the fees. This was in early 1882 when Pearson was 16 and had been at the school for only two years.[7]

Two years later, on 31 May 1884, while Pearson was waiting for confirmation of a promised vacancy at a City of London bank, the prospect of which, in his words, 'did not appeal to me at all',[8] he noticed an advertisement on *Tit-Bits*' front page, in which 'AN EXTRAORDINARY PRIZE' was offered—namely:

> A SITUATION [i.e. job]
> in the Offices of *Tit-Bits*,
> at a Salary of £100 per annum.

To win the prize it was necessary to answer questions on general knowledge, ten of which would appear in each of the next thirteen editions. Pearson said:

> My father's library contained more books of reference than would have been found in most country rectories, but they were quite inadequate when it came to answering the very varied questions which were set to competitors.

However, there was an 'excellent reference department in the Bedford Free Library thirty miles away', to which he journeyed by bicycle three times per week for several weeks.[9]

On 26 September 1884 the result of the competition was announced. Out of 3,000 or so competitors, Pearson had won with 86 correct answers out of a possible 130. That same month he took lodgings in Wimbledon, and the 'shy youth of eighteen',[10] as he described himself, commenced work for George Newnes as office manager at his publishing house in London for a salary not of £100, but of £350 per annum. (*Tit-Bits* had become so successful that its editorial office had been relocated to the capital.)

Pearson was a great success. Before long, Newnes described him as his 'right-hand man' and he was awarded his own private secretary, Ernest Kessell, who had only recently left school.[11] Pearson now began to display that caring side of his nature which would become his hallmark.

> [In his spare time] he would hire an omnibus, into which he would personally pack a company of poor London children, and send them up for a blow on Hampstead Heath. It was part of his nature to love and cheer little children.[12]

Three decades later, a far greater challenge would confront him, as will be seen shortly.

Six months after Pearson joined *Tit-Bits*, its manager suddenly resigned. Pearson applied for the position, but was refused. Three months later, he applied again. Newnes was hesitant, yet in another three months, Pearson's wish was granted.

The energetic Pearson continued to write articles, choosing such varied subjects as 'Fireplaces', 'Echoes', 'Royal Authors', 'Steeplejacks', 'Gout', 'Suspended Animation', 'Duelling', and even 'Rats', and he went to great lengths to get his works published. Said his friend and biographer Sidney Dark, 'there can hardly have been a newspaper or periodical editor in London whom he did not bombard.'[13] A measure of Pearson's success and determination is indicated by his own records which show that in the first half of 1889, no less than fifty-eight out of eighty-four articles written by him were accepted and published—from which he earned the sum of £44.

In December 1887, when Pearson was aged only twenty-one, he married Isobel Sarah, who, like himself, was the offspring of a clergyman—the Reverend John Bennett of Maddington, Wiltshire. Isobel bore him three daughters: Isla, Muriel, and Nora (known as 'Pansy' or 'Pan').[14]

W. T. Stead was editor of the *Pall Mall Gazette*, and in 1889, in partnership with George Newnes, he founded the *Review of Reviews*. Pearson, in his new role as business manager for the *Review of Reviews*, was dispatched to the USA to arrange for the monthly journal to be sold there. Pearson believed that this merited a rise in his salary, but Newnes refused. So, having worked for the company for almost six years, he decided to leave, as did his secretary Ernest Kessell, and the editor, Peter Keary.

Pearson's Weekly

With the help of his two former colleagues from Newnes, Pearson created his own company, C. Arthur Pearson Ltd. Within three weeks, with finance provided by Stephen Mills, the new company published the first number of the periodical journal *Pearson's Weekly*, which appeared on 26 July 1890.

Pearson was known by his friends and colleagues for being extraordinarily dedicated to his work, and to have some rather eccentric habits:

> He had a thick crop of wiry black hair, gold pince-nez glasses, and a small dark moustache. He was totally indifferent to dress, and usually wore, at his office, a Norfolk jacket and a pique four-in-hand tie with a gold pin. He would not always dress for dinner if he could escape the necessity. If he smoked at all, it was very seldom. Experiments and diets interested him. For long periods he would drink nothing but water; eat only fruit for breakfast, and again in the afternoon, when others were taking tea.[1]
>
> He was a man of immense energy. When he first started in business on his own, for the first week in his office, the only sleep he took was on the office table. He literally worked day and night.[2]

The first issue of *Pearson's Weekly* sold a quarter of a million copies. In that same year, 1890, Pearson moved from Wimbledon Common to 'The Bungalow', Shere, in Surrey.[3]

The motto of *Pearson's Weekly* was 'To Interest, to Elevate, to Amuse'. The newspaper was unique in that, unlike all similar publications, it carried no advertisements on its front page. Britain was, at that time, engaged in a war in South Africa and it was not difficult to fill pages with news. Pearson was determined that it would be a cut above other newspapers, with factual and informative articles, debates on topical questions of the day, fictional stories, a letters page where readers could express their views, and competitions for which prizes were awarded.

Mindful, undoubtedly, of the fact that his eyesight was continuing to fail, the twenty-four-year-old Pearson produced an article for the very first edition of *Pearson's Weekly* entitled 'Curiosities of Blindness':

> Appalling as the deprivation of sight may be, it is not without some remarkable compensations. Other faculties, both of intellect and of sense, often seem to gain by it.... Profound thinkers practically admit that vision interferes somewhat with deep cogitation....

Men of genius have sometimes thrown off some of the worst disabilities of blindness. Genius ever devises ways and means of its own. It has a thousand little contrivances unknown to the ordinary student, who is content enough to travel along the beaten road which others have fashioned for him.

He proceeded to give as examples, Nicholas Saunderson, the blind mathematician who became a friend of Sir Isaac Newton and was elected Professor of Mathematics at Cambridge University; John Metcalf, the blind engineer who 'constructed roads through the wilds of Derbyshire'; and Thomas Blacklock, the blind poet and musician who could speak four languages.

Once again demonstrating his caring and philanthropic nature, Pearson, within 18 months of the publication of the first *Pearson's Weekly*, had collected sufficient funds from his readers to enable him to provide a Christmas dinner for many hundreds of deprived children from London's East End.

Pearson resorted to many ingenious ploys in order to keep his readership interested. For example, the first 'happy father' who informed *Pearson's Weekly* that his wife had produced twins, was eligible for the prize of £10, which was awarded weekly for four weeks—provided, of course, that the event was confirmed by a birth certificate. From here, Pearson proceeded to anticipate the modern phenomenon of newspaper dating, when his single young men and women readers were invited to send in a photograph with a reference. The editor then chose a 'lucky young woman' who was given the choice of ten male applicants, similarly selected, to be her husband. She would also receive £100 a year for life, together with the expenses of her wedding and honeymoon.

Other periodicals followed in the wake of *Pearson's Weekly*: *Home Notes*; *The Royal Magazine*; *The Smallholder*; *The Scout* (about which more will be said shortly); *Peg's Paper*; and *Peg's Companion*. 1896 saw the appearance of the pro-socialist *Pearson's Magazine*, which published articles and short stories by such authors as H. G. Wells, George Bernard Shaw, Maxim Gorky, Upton Sinclair, and H. Rider Haggard. Like *Pearson's Weekly*, it also contained articles on science, sport, travel, and invention. In 1899, *Pearson's Magazine* was first published in the USA.

In publishing enterprises such as these, and in another upon which he was soon to embark—namely the launch of the *Daily Express* newspaper—Pearson honed his skills as a great publicist, communicator, and salesman. However, unbeknown to him, it was not in the field of publishing that his achievements were to reach their apotheosis, but in an altogether different enterprise, as will shortly be seen.

Pearson's Fresh Air Fund

In 1892, Pearson launched the Fresh Air Fund, of which he became president. In so doing, he was no doubt aware that he was emulating the Reverend Willard Parsons of Sherman, Pennsylvania, who in 1877 had founded the American prototype of this organization. Writing about the fund in the April edition of *Pearson's Weekly*, Pearson declared,

> We are very anxious to make arrangements which, during the coming summer, will result in many poor London children having a breath of pure country air which to most of them is such a rarity. We believe that we shall be able to arrange for children to have a day in the country within a radius of 20 miles of London for 9*d* [nine pence] a head. This sum including railway fares and a supply of good food. Now what we have set our hearts on is to raise enough money to enable us to send a party of 2,000 children away for a day's outing every weekday between June 13th and September 17th!

The response was enthusiastic:

> A generous public immediately forwarded subscriptions … to such an extent that the first party of 2,000 children were taken to Snaresbrook on the outskirts of Epping Forest on June 15th 1892.[1]

When Pearson founded the *Daily Express* in 1900 (about which more will be said shortly) and subsequently took control of a number of other newspapers, he was able to use these publications—in addition to *Pearson's Weekly*—as a vehicle to advertise the project. By the following year, no less than twenty-nine cities and towns in the United Kingdom had been incorporated into the Fresh Air Fund.

Pearson revealed just how much he empathized with these 'thousands of little children in our great cities who never see the country and never breathe the fresh air':

> The scent of hayfields, the shaded hedgerows, diversified with fragrant flowers, the peaceful woodlands, are all unknown to them. They never bathe their feet in the running stream, nor see the butterflies [a poignant comment, for one who was losing his sight] nor hear the birds singing. They do not know the joy of living. How good a thing it was to hear the laughter of the city children at play in the meadows and woods—to let them feast 'al fresco' to their small hearts' content on wholesome country fare.

And yet he was not satisfied. One day's holiday was not enough, said he: 'I should like every child to be away for at least two weeks'.[2] By the end of the first decade of the Fund's life, no less than 767,625 children had enjoyed a day out in the countryside.

In 1910, King George V assented to become the Fresh Air Fund's Patron. Pearson said, 'The fund this year took from town to country a little army of 6,000 cripples, and there also went, for the fresh air holidays 1,000 blind children.'[3]

Soon, and in very different circumstances, Pearson would have the opportunity to demonstrate his concern for the blind, not only nationally, but on the world stage.

Pearson Remarries: Frensham Place

In 1897 Pearson's marriage to Isobel was dissolved. Now a wealthy thirty-one-year-old, in June of the same year, he married Ethel Maud, daughter of William John Fraser Esquire of 'Cromartie', Herne Bay, Kent. By her he had a son, Neville Arthur, born on 13 February 1898.

In the face of her husband's deteriorating eyesight, Ethel would prove to be a steadfast ally. Not only that, when he embarked on the greatest enterprise of his life, one of which he had at present no inkling, she would be there at his side, offering not only emotional support, but also practical assistance.

The couple set up home at Frensham Place in Farnham, Surrey. The elegant mansion boasted a ballroom, and its estate of 120 acres included a farm, granary, orchard, kitchen gardens, park, stables, pleasure gardens, a lake, and pine woods. Here, Pearson laid out an 18-hole golf course, established an indoor riding school, and converted part of the stables into an aviary in which he kept his collection of rare birds. He also kept bees and planted lavender bushes in profusion in order to provide the bees with nectar.

Pearson commuted back and forth to his office in London, but he would never allow himself an idle moment, as attested by a colleague of his, who preferred to remain anonymous:

> [He] never wasted a moment of the long train journey to Town. When the return journey was made in the dark he would still work on manuscripts and proofs, using a little lamp fastened in the buttonhole of his coat, so that he could read.

In his hours of leisure, said the colleague, he was equally strenuous:

> [He was] always ready to take up something new. When he began keeping horses, he started at once to drive a tandem and a four-in-hand without any previous experience. He trusted to his own judgment and skill. His only accident, it is recorded, was when the front part of a wagonette broke away from the body of the carriage and Mr Pearson, who was driving a spirited pair of horses, refusing to let go of the reigns, was dragged a long distance down the road. For a time he was laid up for his injuries, but he was compensated for his inaction by thinking that the horses had not got away from him!

Pearson cared little for art or music. He was an outdoor type who enjoyed caravanning holidays and collecting ivory carvings.[1] When motor cars became popular, Pearson was only

Lady Pearson (Ethel Fraser) by
P. L. J. Morris. (*The Hon. Mrs
Egerton-Warburton*)

interested in the high-powered variety, which he 'drove with characteristic recklessness'.[2] He also enjoyed a round of golf, but sadly, in the words of journalist, art collector, and historian Bernard Falk: 'It was while playing golf at Frensham near Farnham, that he first realized that he was going blind. He could no longer see the ball.'[3]

Pearson the Newspaper Proprietor

Having witnessed the success of Lord Northcliffe's *Daily Mail*, founded by in 1896, Pearson decided to found a newspaper of his own. It would be called the *Daily Express*. However, in order for the launch to go well, it was necessary to achieve a 'scoop'—something both 'fresh and striking', to attract the attention of potential readers. He therefore sent for Hesketh V. H. Prichard, who at the age of twenty-two, was already a Fellow of both the Royal Geographical Society and the Zoological Society. Pearson offered to finance an expedition to the Caribbean island of Haiti, with Prichard as its leader:

> No white man had crossed Haiti, or indeed, had travelled into the interior for a hundred years, since the blacks in 1803 revolted against the French settlers and massacred them. [To date] All that had come to the outer world from Haiti were rumours... of snake-worship and poisonings, human sacrifice and cannibalism.[1]

Having agreed to Pearson's suggestion, Prichard arrived in Haiti in November 1899.

Publication of the *Daily Express*, which cost one halfpenny per copy (and into which the *Morning Herald*, which Pearson had acquired in 1898, was merged), duly commenced in April 1900. Its battle-cry was 'Truth and Right, Independence, Sympathy, Justice for All', and Pearson was its first editor. Furthermore, the front page of the very first issue of the newspaper, dated Tuesday 24 April, contained an invitation to the reader to enjoy the first of a series of articles by Mr Hesketh Prichard concerning his visit to 'Hayti [Haiti], the Black Republic'. Readers were assured that Prichard's revelations in regard to the island would 'undoubtedly afford a world sensation'.

The front page also contained news of the British Empire, and a personal message sent to the *Daily Express* by none other than the German Emperor Wilhelm II (known as 'The Kaiser'). It read as follows:

> I offer my good wishes for the success of the 'Daily Express', which, as I understand, proposes to foster that most excellent of missions, the promotion of international goodwill.
>
> Tell the British people that my first hope, now and always, is the preservation of international peace; my second, the consolidation and maintenance of good relations between Germany and Great Britain.
>
> Between these two nations no essential cause of difference exists, nor should one arise between them. There should be no rivalry, other than friendly competition in furthering the economic and social progress of their peoples.

Hesketh V. H. Prichard. (*Charlie Jacoby*)

The irony, of course, would only have become apparent years later. Other news included that of the progress of the Boer War.

On 22 January 1901, Pearson was almost responsible for the demise of his own newspaper. The long reign of the sovereign, Queen Victoria, was coming to a close. She was gravely ill at Osborne House—her royal residence on the Isle of Wight—and her death was expected imminently.

> It was for that moment that Pearson made his preparations. When the Great Queen passed away, a handkerchief was to be waved from a window in Osborne, [whereupon] a pigeon was to be released for flight to Portsmouth [on the mainland], and thence a telephone to London would launch upon the Empire myriads of cables giving the momentous news.

However, only five minutes after the plan had been executed, Pearson received a telephone call: 'News uncertain, detain cables.' Pearson feared that his *Daily Express* would surely 'expire from ridicule' and was therefore, 'in perfect agony'. Another ten 'interminable minutes' passed. Then further news of the Queen arrived. Yes, she *had* indeed passed away, 'and Pearson and his paper lived again'.[2]

On Thursday 14 June 1901, Pearson arrived in New York, having crossed the Atlantic Ocean on the White Star liner *Oceanic*. Said a *New York Times* reporter:

> He is on a pleasure trip, but will look after the interests of his publications in the United States. His stay will be but ten days, and he is to visit the Pan-American Exposition at Buffalo and Philadelphia.

This was Pearson's fifth visit to the USA. *Pearson's Magazine*, he declared, had sold more copies in that country than it had sold at home in the UK. Said he, 'I am going to try and discover why the magazine sells so well—too well—in America and put the knowledge to good use when I return.' As for the *Daily Express*, he was proud to say, 'we print more American news than any other English newspaper. We have of course a special service from our New York correspondent. [However] I do not intend to Americanize the *Express*.' As for the future, he was full of enthusiasm:

> I have another project, not worked out... to establish a chain of papers around the world. The plan at present is to have one at Montreal, in Bombay and Calcutta in India, at Cape Town, and at Melbourne, Australia.

Finally, the *New York Times* reported on Pearson's charitable interests:

> Mr Pearson appeared to be very much interested in New York's Fresh Air Funds and their scope and management. His publications have in the last five years collected enough to give 750,000 children a Summer outing.[3]

It was as a result of a meeting, in July 1903, between Pearson and Conservative politician and Colonial Secretary Joseph Chamberlain, that the Tariff Reform League was created with Pearson as its chairman. Its objective was to establish a single trading bloc within the British Empire, and to impose tariffs on goods entering it from the rest of the world.

In 1903, Pearson acquired the *St James's Gazette*. In 1904 he purchased *The Standard* and its sister newspaper *The Evening Standard* (which he amalgamated with the *St James's Gazette*), and changed the stance of both newspapers from pro-Conservative to pro-Liberal.

That Christmas, Pearson's colleagues presented him with a French clock. It bore the inscription

The

Daily Express

To

CAP

Xmas 1904

Lest you forget

[i.e. lest he forget his colleagues, who had given him the clock in appreciation.]

Sadly, over the course of the next few years, Pearson's eyesight continued to deteriorate. He had been diagnosed as suffering from glaucoma—a disease in which the pressure within the eyeballs rises unduly and destroys the optic nerves. In March 1908 he underwent surgery. (Today, glaucoma would be treated, initially with pressure-relieving eye drops.) The operation, performed by Mr Robert Doyne, was not a lasting success and soon Pearson was unable to see well enough either to read or to write.

Two years later he took his wife Ethel and their children to the Continent—to Switzerland in particular. He was determined that if blindness was to overtake him, which seemed

The clock presented to Pearson by his colleagues at the *Daily Express*, Christmas 1904. (*The Hon. Mrs Egerton-Warburton*)

inevitable, then he would first see as much of that beautiful country as he could. To assist them on their journey they took with them *Bradshaw's Continental Railway Guide*.[4]

Sales in *The Standard* and *The Evening Standard* declined, and in 1910 Pearson sold them both. An attempt by him to take over *The Times* was also unsuccessful. Nevertheless, he acquired a controlling interest in many provincial newspapers, including the *Birmingham Daily Gazette*, the *Leicester Evening News*, the *North Mail*, the *Midland Express*, and the *Newcastle Weekly Leader*. Meanwhile, his company, C. Arthur Pearson Ltd, continued to flourish, as did *Pearson's Magazine*.

As time went by, Pearson found himself devoting more of his time to his pursuits at Frensham Place and less to his business empire. He enjoyed riding in the woods, driving horses, boating, and swimming in the lake. This life of idyllic rusticity, however, was interspersed with episodes of furious activity.

6

Pearson and the Search for
the Giant Sloth

The *Daily Express* edition of 22 June 1900 carried the following headline:

GIANT SLOTH OF PATAGONIA
A NEW 'EXPRESS' SCIENTIFIC EXPEDITION

In anticipation of achieving another scoop for his newspaper, Pearson intended to send Hesketh Prichard on another expedition. This time it would be to Patagonia. Pearson hoped that Prichard would discover a living example of a megatherium, or giant ground sloth (a large, hairy, bear-like creature now believed to be extinct).[1]   In Prichard's words,

> Mr Pearson, the proprietor of the *Daily Express*, most generously financed the Expedition in the interests of science, and entrusted me with the task of sifting all the evidence for or against the chances of survival [of the megatherium] obtainable on the spot.[2]

Seven decades previously, in 1831, English naturalist Charles Darwin had travelled on the ship HMS *Beagle*. Her captain was Robert Fitzroy, whose task it was to make a scientific survey of South American waters. During the expedition, several visits were made to Punta Alta on Argentina's Atlantic coast, where many bones were to be found wedged in the cliffs. On one such visit, Darwin found an almost complete skeleton of a megatherium, which he presented to Dr Richard Owen, Conservator of London's Hunterian Museum.[3]

Owen not only confirmed the identity of the skeleton, he reconstructed it and displayed it in his museum raised up on its hind legs, and grasping a tree trunk with its forelegs. From its size and shape, it was clear that the megatherium was one of the largest mammals ever to walk the earth—weighing as much as an African bull elephant, viz. in excess of 4 tons.

The party, led by Prichard, consisted of eight men, sixty horses, a waggon, and a boat. Having arrived at Puerto Madryn, Argentina, in September 1900, it set out on a journey westwards towards the Andes mountains. Prichard kept a diary, extracts from which were sent back to England at regular intervals to be printed in the *Daily Express* and read avidly by its readers. Was it possible that, somewhere in the remote lands of South America, a living megatherium would be found? This was the question which gripped not only the readers of the *Daily Express*, but the whole country, which was set ablaze with 'giant sloth fever'!

Despite journeying 1,750 miles overland, Prichard found no trace of his quarry. However, high in the Chilean Andes, north of Lake Argentino, he discovered a lake, which he named

Lake Pearson, after his sponsor. He set sail for home from Punta Arenas in the far south of Chile in late May 1901, bringing with him many artefacts, including the skin of a puma, which he presented (on Pearson's behalf) to the Natural History Museum. Here, it was examined by Oldfield Thomas, Fellow of the Royal Society, who declared that the skin, which was 'remarkably unlike [that of] any known form of puma,' was of a sub-species of *Felis concolor puma*. Furthermore, said he, 'In commemoration of Mr Pearson's scientific spirit in sending out the expedition … I would propose to call it *Felis concolor Pearsoni*.'[4]

Felis concolor pearsoni—'Pearson's Puma' by John Guille Millais.

C. Arthur Pearson Ltd

In the early 1900s, Pearson's company, C. Arthur Pearson Ltd, published a series of guide books featuring cities such as Edinburgh, London, and Paris; also, the County of Devonshire and the English Lake District. Pearson also published historical novels, *Handbooks on Useful Hobbies*, and *Handbooks of General Information*. In fact, the magazine contained something for everyone: man or woman, upper or lower class, urbanite or country-dwellers. Even courting couples could avail themselves of *The Lovers' Guide*, and for the prospective parent there was *Names for Baby*.

Interestingly, C. Arthur Pearson Ltd published a large selection of books on the occult (defined as concerned with the supernatural, mystical, magical[1]), four of which were written by Pearson, all in 1902 when he was aged thirty-six, and all under the pseudonym 'Professor P. R. S. Foli'. They were *Pearson's Dream Book*, *Pearson's Fortune Teller*, *Fortune Telling By Cards*, and *Handwriting as an Index to Character*.

Despite his great success as a self-made newspaper proprietor, Pearson's lifestyle options were becoming increasingly circumscribed as his eyesight gradually failed and darkness inexorably closed in. This begs the question, as he teetered on the edge of darkness, did his interest in the occult arise in part from a desperate desire to discover, by a study of the supernatural, what his own future had in store for him?

Pearson and the Scout Movement

When Robert S. S. Baden-Powell (1857–1941) had the idea of creating the Scout Movement, Pearson was the first person to whom he turned for advice.

Baden-Powell was the sixth son of the Reverend H. G. Baden-Powell, Professor of Geometry at Oxford University, who had died when Robert was only three years old. The latter's interest in scouting and woodcraft had begun when he was at school at Charterhouse in Surrey, where, in his spare time, he would play in the woods, practise stalking, and catch and cook rabbits. On holiday he was equally adventurous: sailing in a yacht round the southern coast of England, and canoeing along the River Thames. When he left school he joined the army and served in India and Afghanistan. He had become famous for having organized the successful defence of Mafeking by the British during the Boer War. He had returned to England in 1903 and was appointed Inspector-General of Cavalry. His thoughts now turned to the young people of his native land.

During his time in the army as a Major General, Baden-Powell had written several military training manuals including *Reconnaissance and Scouting* (1884) and *Aids to Scouting for NCOs and Men* (1899). In 1904, Scottish businessman William A. Smith (later Sir William), founder of the Boys' Brigade, suggested to him that he write a similar manual designed to be read and used by a younger audience. The outcome was that in 1906, Baden-Powell sent Smith a short article entitled 'Scouting for Boys', which was published that June in the *Boys' Brigade Gazette*.

In July 1906, Baden-Powell was invited by Pearson to Frensham Place. 'Here is the man I want to help me,' he said '—a lover of children, a famous organizer; a great publicity man; he will know how best to start.'[1] At dinner, Baden-Powell elaborated on his concerns for the youth of the land, many of whom, through a lack of education, proper parenting, self-discipline, and moral guidance, would surely find themselves ill-equipped for the workplace and unlikely to hold down a steady job. 'There are one and three-quarter million boys in the country at present outside the range of good influences,' he said, 'mostly drifting towards hooliganism, for want of a helping hand.'[2] He proceeded to explain to Pearson how he proposed to make use of his experience of training scouts in the army to benefit the youth of Britain. Finally, between them, the two men came up with a name for the proposed new organization—the 'Boy Scout' movement.[3] It was also agreed that Baden-Powell would produce a new manual, entitled *Scouting for Boys*.

When, from 25 July to 9 August 1907, with the permission of its owner Charles van Raalte, Baden-Powell held an experimental scout camp on Brownsea Island in Poole Harbour, Dorset, where he had sailed with his brothers as a boy, Pearson assigned his Editor-in-Chief Percy W. Everett to attend for the final four days in the role of Assistant Scout Master. Said Everett:

We just imagined a set of boys having a good time on the Island…. Well, this is what it was but it was something much more. A trail was being laid at that camp, to be followed by boys and girls that would reach round the world.[4]

Scouting for Boys was published, priced 4*d* per issue (each of which was about 70 pages in length) on six alternate Wednesdays, commencing on 15 January 1908. It was produced by Horace Cox, printers to C. Arthur Pearson Ltd. In this, Pearson himself was heavily involved, both in designing its format and in managing its promotion and marketing.

The success of *Scouting for Boys* surprised everybody, and when the popular edition was published it sold at the rate of 5,000 copies per month and was reprinted five times in one year, eventually becoming one of the best-selling books of the twentieth century and being translated into numerous languages. For the scouting movement, the outcome was entirely predictable. All over the country, hundreds of scout troops sprung up, both of boys and (perhaps to Baden-Powell's surprise) of girls.

On 14 April 1908, the first issue of *The Scout*, a weekly newspaper for boys, was published. The Girl Guide Movement was founded in 1910 and Baden-Powell was obliged to formulate, hastily, the rules and regulations of the Movement—which he did almost overnight. In that year, Pearson sold both the *Evening Standard* and the *Standard*.

On 24 January 1912, Pearson's son Neville commenced as a pupil at Eton College. Here, he would display the same athletic prowess as his paternal forebears, excelling at cricket and also at Fives.

On 26 May 1912, Pearson wrote to Hesketh Prichard to appraise him of how matters stood in regard to his failing eyesight. Never one to complain, the former was clearly at a low ebb:

I am very much under the weather. The retina of my left eye has split, for some unexplainable reason, and to all intents and purposes depriving that eye of sight, for I only see with it what I can see with my right eye. I have been flat on my back with eyes bandaged for a fortnight now, and have another fortnight of the same joy to look forward to. This is said to be my only chance of saving my sight at all in my left eye, and I want to, as the right one is a very poor creature.[5]

In that year, Conservative politician and businessman Max Aitken (who received a peerage in 1917 and became the 1st Baron Beaverbrook) lent money to the *Daily Express* enterprise—the newspaper being in financial difficulty.

Lord Baden-Powell. (*The Scout Association*)

Pearson and
the National Institute for the Blind

In 1913, Pearson was informed by Professor Ernst Fuchs of Vienna that he would soon be blind, so in that year he disposed of his remaining interests in publishing. He now required a project in which to immerse himself and channel his prodigious energies. Accordingly, that October, shortly before his eyesight failed him completely, Pearson joined the Council of the British and Foreign Society for Improving the Embossed Literature for the Blind. This was based on a system developed by French educationist Louis Braille (1809–52), who had himself become blind when only four years old as a result of an accident in his father's shoemaker's workshop. In January 1914, Pearson became the society's treasurer. According to Sidney Dark,

> Pearson ... took a definite and particular interest in the printing and publishing of embossed literature for the blind both in the Braille and Moon types [William Moon, blind inventor and teacher of the blind, who devised a system based on embossed roman capitals, which is easier to read than Braille, but which occupies more space on the page] with the result that the supply has enormously increased of late years, both in quantity and variety, to the infinite advantage and pleasure of the blind.[1]

Early in 1914, the society relocated from London's Cambridge Square (the home of one of the organization's co-founders, Dr Thomas Rhodes Armitage) to new premises in Great Portland Street. These were officially opened on 19 March by His Majesty King George V. £30,000 was required to equip the building and, in particular, to enlarge its library of Braille books and to create an endowment fund for their further manufacture. In July 1914, Pearson was elected the society's first president, and the organization would from henceforth be known as the National Institute for the Blind (NIB).

> King George, in opening the new premises of the National Institute for the Blind, wished God-speed to the appeal for books in Braille for the sightless, which His Majesty said would, 'break down the barriers shutting out the blind from the common interests of life. I am confident your appeal for funds will stir the imagination of many who unreflectingly enjoy the blessings of sight.'[2]

Pearson set about raising the money required in a typically imaginative way: by arranging with the Marconi Telegraph Company for the following appeal to be made by their wireless operator at Poldhu, Cornwall, to every ship that he could trace travelling up and down the English Channel.

> Books in Braille are practically the only solace of the blind, and, in view of His Majesty's speech, which guarantees the genuineness and urgency of this appeal, may we ask you to arrange during the voyage subscriptions to this first appeal on record made by wireless. The appeal is made to all on board British ships, and even [to] the sympathetic friends on ships flying other flags who are grateful that they are not blind. Kindly send the proceeds to the Lord Mayor's Fund for the Blind, Mansion House, London. This message sent to you gratis by the kindness of the Marconi [Wireless] Company.[3]

Pearson, it will be remembered, had given Baden-Powell considerable assistance in launching his Scout Movement. Now it was time for the favour to be repaid. The outcome was that on 2 May 1914, Baden-Powell made the request that 'All scouts perform a "good turn" for *The Scout* magazine publisher Mr C. Arthur Pearson, in order to raise money for his scheme of publishing literature in Braille for the blind.'

Pearson also enlisted the support of the Mansion House Fund (founded on 29 May 1914 by Sir T. Vansittart Bowater, Lord Mayor of London). Pearson himself contributed the sum of £1,000 from his own pocket, as did newspaper publishing magnates Lord Northcliffe and Lord Rothermere. He also persuaded the Archbishops of Canterbury and Westminster, together with the leaders of the Free Churches, to hold a special service of thanksgiving for the blessing of sight, with the result that over 40,000 such services were held simultaneously throughout the country, and a great deal more money was raised.

When Pearson had joined the NIB, in October 1913, its income was a mere £8,000 per annum—barely sufficient to fund its operations. By 1915 the sum of £60,000 had been raised, and by 1921, the NIB's annual income had risen to £358,174.[4]

Pearson and
the Founding of St Dunstan's

On 4 August 1914, Great Britain declared war on Germany following that country's invasion of neutral Belgium. (This was under the terms of the Treaty of London, 1839.) In the same year, the Prince of Wales asked Pearson to be director of the National Relief Fund, which was committed to alleviating distress among demobilized service personnel. The outcome was that Pearson became Joint Honorary Secretary of that organization's Collecting Committee, and in less than 6 months it had raised the sum of £1,000,000.

Also in 1914 the Pearsons sold Frensham Place and relocated to Bourne End in Hertfordshire. Due to the property having stables and an indoor riding school, his former home was now requisitioned by the military for use as a training centre for recruits to the cavalry.

On 8 September 1914, the Council of the NIB resolved that 'steps should be taken to make it known that the Institute would, as far as practicable, help such men as lose their sight whilst on service in the war'.[1]

On Friday 29 January 1915 at York House, St James's Palace, Pearson convened a meeting. It was attended by himself, Miss Ethel W. Austin, Secretary of the National Library for the Blind, P. Tindal Robertson Esq. of the British Red Cross, and Henry Stainsby Esq., Secretary of the NIB. Pearson opened the proceedings by outlining what the NIB planned to do to help those blinded during the war. He said

> a number of Soldiers had been blinded in the War, that the National Institute [for the Blind] was in touch with twenty two of these and there would be doubtless more such cases all requiring to be promptly and sympathetically dealt with. They should be taught to read & write in the embossed type, assisted to acquire some occupation and generally trained to become active, self-reliant and self-helpful.

In order that this might be accomplished it was thought 'highly desirable that a Convalescent Home should be established, equipped and maintained wherein such training could be carried out'.

The British Red Cross Society, said Pearson, was 'cordially in agreement with the suggestion,' as was the Council of the National Institute for the Blind [NIB]. He therefore proposed to constitute a committee, with himself as Chairman. It would consist of those present together with the British Red Cross Society's chairman the Hon. Arthur Stanley, and Captain Ernest B. B. Towse. Towse had been blinded while serving with the Gordon Highlanders during the Boer War, in which he had been awarded the Victoria Cross (VC) for valour. Finally, Pearson produced a letter from His Majesty the King, 'expressing warm approval of the scheme'.[2]

From henceforth, the Committee would meet on a regular basis, usually every week to ten days. Said Pearson:

> I had the conviction that the usual attitude towards the blind was very mistaken; so much talk of pity, of their affliction; so many things said and done to make them feel a people apart.
>
> I went to see in Hospital the first blinded soldier to be brought back from the front, and it was then I formed the plans which were soon to be carried out at St Dunstans. The essential idea was that blindness should be regarded only as a handicap, that the blinded men should be encouraged to forget what they couldn't do, and to be swiftly interested in what they could do, that they should feel themselves still in close touch with the ordinary interests of life; that they should be treated and should bear themselves as nearly as might be, like normal people.[3]

In order that no war-blinded serviceman should be overlooked, Pearson enlisted the cooperation of Surgeon-General Sir Alfred Keogh, and 'thereafter every effort was made to send all the blinded men when they reached England to the 2nd London General Hospital'. This hospital, located in Chelsea, had been St Mark's before the war, a teacher training college run by the Church's National Society.[4] Said Pearson:

> At least once a week it was my practice to visit the hospital, to see especially the men who had newly arrived. I felt that because I too was blind I might speak to these men of their future more convincingly than if I had not shared the same experience and faced the same problems.[5]
>
> The main idea that animated me in establishing this hostel for the blinded soldiers was that the sightless men, after being discharged from hospital, might come into a little world where the things which blind men cannot do, were forgotten and where everyone was concerned with what blind men can do. They would naturally need to be looked after and to be trained, and I was convinced that their future happiness, their success, everything, in short, would depend on the atmosphere with which they were surrounded....[6]
>
> With practically no exceptions all the soldiers and sailors of the British Imperial Forces blinded in the war came under my care, in order that they might learn to be blind.[7]

(In fact, a small number of blinded airmen were also catered for.)

German banker and patron of the arts, Otto Hermann Kahn now unexpectedly intervened. Kahn was born in Mannheim, Germany, in 1867. In 1888 he relocated to London, where he worked for Berlin's Deutsche Bank; he also became a British citizen. In 1893, he moved to New York City where he joined Kuhn, Loeb & Co.—a firm of investment bankers. He was in two minds, however, about whether or not to return to England.

Max Aitken suggested to Kahn that if, as a foreigner and a Jew, he wished to be accepted into the life of the City of London, there were two things which it would be advisable for him to do. The first was to stand for Parliament, and the second was to purchase Pearson's *Daily Express* newspaper which, as already mentioned, was in financial difficulty. Kahn and Pearson met, and the former went so far as to offer the latter the sum of £30,000 for the newspaper. He then had second thoughts, both about this venture and about a career in politics, and decided to remain in the USA. Nevertheless, he retained his home, 'St Dunstan's in London's Regent's

Otto Kahn.

Park, which he had rented from Henry Hucks Gibbs (1st Lord Altringham) since 1912. This was a large mansion once owned by the 3rd Marquis of Hertford, designed by the famous architect Decimus Burton and built at the time of the Regency (1810–20).

Having heard that Pearson was seeking premises for his blinded men, Kahn generously offered to place St Dunstan's at his disposal. This was completely free of all charges, including the cost of maintenance of the grounds, and to some extent of the house itself. Kahn also contributed generously to the hostel's general fund. Pearson's friend and biographer, Sidney Dark, was very enthusiastic about the location: 'St Dunstan's has all the advantages of a large country house with a wonderful garden, though it is within a couple of miles of Central London's Piccadilly Circus.'[8] In fact, the garden was of 15 acres and second in size only to that of Buckingham Palace! It included a lake, which was contiguous with the larger one in nearby Regent's Park.

At a subsequent meeting of the Committee, held on 2 February 1915, it was resolved that Otto Kahn's generous offer be gratefully accepted. However, as St Dunstan's, Regent's Park, was not yet ready for occupation, it was deemed necessary to find alternative accommodation in the meantime.

Mrs Lewis Hall, subsequently described by Pearson as 'a continuous benefactor to the blinded men,' now came to the rescue by placing No. 6 Bayswater Hill at the disposal of the Committee. This would provide accommodation for fourteen residents.[9]

On 5 February 1915, even before Bayswater Hill had opened its doors, Dr D. R. Arnold Lawson and Mr J. M. Sandwich were appointed honorary ophthalmic advisors, Miss F. A. Davy was appointed Matron, and Mr Oscar Ballantine was made Secretary. It was also agreed that the Voluntary Aid Detachment ('VAD')—created by the Red Cross prior to the First World War—would undertake 'sundry house duties'. Finally, Pearson stated that he had asked the Committee of the National Relief Fund 'to make a grant of £1000 for the upkeep of the Home and £4000 to be used for the betterment and welfare of the blinded soldiers after they had been discharged from the Home.'[10]

No. 6 Bayswater Hill, The Blinded Soldiers & Sailors Hostel, February 1915. (*Blind Veterans UK*)

On 9 February 1915 it was resolved that the home would be named the 'Blinded Soldiers & Sailors Hostel' and that the Committee would be known as the 'Blinded Soldiers & Sailors Care Committee'. Two 'teachers and general helpers' were appointed: Miss D. A. Pain and Miss G. Heckrath, together with two orderlies. Dr A. Washington G. Ranger, a close friend of Pearson, was also invited to join the Committee.[11] Washington Ranger (born 1849) had graduated in law from Oxford University despite being blind from the age of fourteen, and had founded the legal firm Ranger, Burton & Frost. Pearson subsequently described Washington Ranger as a 'tireless supporter' in respect of the former's efforts on behalf of the blind. The following day, 10 February, the Blinded Soldiers & Sailors Hostel, 6 Baywater Hill, admitted its first war-blinded man—John Batchelor of the 3rd Royal Sussex Regiment, a regular soldier who was wounded at Ypres in October 1914.

On 18 February 1915, Pearson informed the Committee that he had received a letter from Queen Mary, wife of the Sovereign King George V, in which Her Majesty had expressed her 'sympathetic interest in the work this Committee was doing'.[12]

When the Committee convened again on 25 February 1915, it was to learn that several generous gestures had been made. Mr Swinnerton of Newport in Wales had offered to provide 'a country house for short stay visits of the blinded soldiers and sailors'; Mrs Burden Muller of 12 Portland Square would provide accommodation for 'relatives of the blinded soldiers who came from the country to make their visits to the men'; and a Mr Sidney Parry had donated prizes for 'Braille efficiency'.

A dentist was appointed, and two blinded soldiers (Davie and Johnstone) were to be transferred from the NIB to serve 'as travellers & assistants to the hostel at wages of 35/- per

St Dunstan's, Regent's Park. (*Blind Veterans UK*)

week each'. Also, each resident of the hostel would be entitled to receive up to seven visitors per week to tea.[13]

By 4 March 1915 there were eight blinded soldiers in residence at the hostel, and a further five had accepted invitations, but there had also been five refusals. Meanwhile, ten men were still in hospital and (presumably) awaiting admission to the hostel, three of them having recovered their sight in one eye. There was also mention of 'two Belgians [servicemen] whose whereabouts were uncertain'.

Pearson reported further manifestations of goodwill towards the blinded men: 'Homes for short stays of blinded men with their wives had been offered at Brighton [Sussex] & Torquay [Devonshire].' Meanwhile, the hostel had received in excess of 120 donations, making a total sum of £931 8s 6d.[14]

In March there were further appointments in view: a Mr Mitchell, to teach basketwork,[15] and volunteer Mr Charles E. Rose to be Superintendent of the Workshops.[16]

Finally, on 26 March 1915 the great day came when the Blinded Soldiers & Sailors Hostel relocated from Bayswater to Regent's Park, with Miss J. E. Davidson as its first Matron. Established as a charity and maintained jointly by, and run under the auspices of, the British Red Cross Society, the Order of St John of Jerusalem, and the NIB, and supported by public donations, the hostel was renamed 'St Dunstan's Hostel for Blinded Soldiers and Sailors'. The extra accommodation provided by the new premises was desperately needed, owing to the ever-increasing influx of war blinded. Furthermore, the ballroom of the house would serve as a lounge, and its large conservatory as a classroom/workshop where various handicrafts would be taught.[17]

St Dunstan's, Regent's Park, acquired its name through an extraordinary set of circumstances. In London's Fleet Street stands the Church of St Dunstan-in-the-West. This church possessed a clock (built by Thomas Harrys in 1671) which was attached to the side of the building. The clock was of a substantial size and unique in that it was the first ever made to display the minutes as well as the hours. When the church was refurbished, funds were needed, so the decision was made to sell the clock. It was then purchased by Francis Conway, 3rd Marquis of Hertford for the sum of 200 guineas. He set it up in the grounds of his London residence, which he accordingly renamed 'St Dunstan's'. A feature of the clock were two giant figures, carved in oak, which struck the hours and the quarter hours upon an anvil. The Marquis was particularly fond of it because, as a child, his nanny would take him to see the giants strike the bell as a treat whenever he had been well behaved.[18]

As for St Dunstan himself (909–88), he was Abbot of Glastonbury Abbey in Somersetshire, and from 960, Archbishop of Canterbury. He was subsequently canonized as a saint. Since the Middle Ages, St Dunstan has been regarded as the patron saint of goldsmiths and silversmiths and he is most frequently represented holding a pair of smith's tongs. Who, therefore, is the patron saint of the blind? About this, there is considerable difference of opinion between the various branches of the Christian Church. Main contenders for this honour are St Odelia (French, seventh century), St Lucy (Santa Lucia, Sicilian, third century), St Raphael the Archangel (mentioned in the Holy Bible), St Alice (Belgian, thirteenth century), and the twin brothers St Cosmos and St Damien (Syrian, fourth century). However, in his book *Victory Over Blindness*, Pearson was adamant that St Dunstan had 'become the Patron Saint of the Blinded Soldiers and Sailors'.[19]

The Newcomer to St Dunstan's

What was it like to be a newcomer to St Dunstan's? First, one may picture a visit by Pearson (or a member of his staff, or his daughter Nora, who also helped him in this respect) to the hospital bedside of a newly blinded serviceman, who may well be experiencing emotions such as grief, rage, bitterness, and despair. Therefore, great sensitivity was called for.

Pearson places his cards on the table and offers the man a place at his hostel. He is met with scepticism, but he perseveres. After all, he has done this many times before, and as already mentioned, he is something of an authority on the human mind, having written a number of books on how to gain an insight into a person's character. This will now stand him in good stead. Pearson explains about St Dunstan's. That it is not a home in which people are to be shut away for the rest of their lives. Quite the reverse; the objective is to teach a man a trade, and thus enable him to become independent and stand on his own two feet. Finally, Pearson discloses that he himself is blind.

The man considers the alternatives. Almost invariably, he realizes that there are none. And there is something about this stranger that he feels he can trust. Yet, nagging at the back of his mind is a tiny voice which says, 'How can *he* help *me*? How can *anybody* help *me*?'

Before Pearson leaves the man's bedside there is a ritual to be performed. It is a seemingly small affair, but one which is of great symbolism: he presents the man with a Braille watch (supplied by the NIB). As the man runs his fingers over the object, Pearson explains how it works; how, by turning the winder to a certain position, the case may be opened to expose the dial. Also how, on the dial, numbers are replaced by raised dots, so by feeling where the hands are in relation to them, the time may be ascertained—with the knowledge that the dot at the top beneath the timer represents 12 o'clock. The ability to tell the time, says Pearson, is the very first step on the way to an independent life.

Once the blinded man has accepted Pearson's invitation to St Dunstan's, everything swings into action. Prior to his discharge from hospital, he will receive regular visits from a female tutor (one of dozens who have been recruited by St Dunstan's from the staff of the National Library for the Blind) who will introduce him to Braille and to typewriting, and who will teach him how to make a string bag. She will read his letters to him and help him to write letters of his own. Newsworthy topics of the day will be discussed, in order to keep his mind occupied and keep boredom at bay. This is an essential prelude to the man's rehabilitation, for, as St Dunstan's Consultant Ophthalmologist, Arnold Lawson, pointed out,

Pearson in his office in Regent's Park. (*Blind Veterans UK*)

The sudden plunging of the sighted man into darkness by the havoc of a shell-burst or bullet, must be, and is followed by a period of mental depression often of the most acute character, which persists in many persons for long periods.[1]

On his release from hospital, the blinded serviceman is ferried across London by taxi to St Dunstan's, Regent's Park. Here, he is met by a cadre of Boy Scouts who take care of his luggage, pay his taxi fare, and introduce him to a VAD whose task it is to register new arrivals. He then reports to Matron, who allocates him a bed in a dormitory, shows him where to put his clothes, and reads him the house rules. She introduces him to the Dispensary Nurse who will give him all the necessary attention in respect of his injuries, and then to some of the blind residents who are sitting comfortably in the lounge. Finally, she offers him a meal.

Pearson realized that if he was to have any chance of success with his blinded men, it was first necessary to gain their trust. To this end, on the day following his admission to St Dunstan's, the newcomer receives an invitation from the 'Chief'—as Pearson was known—to see him in his private office at 12 noon. Shortly afterwards, his relatives are also interviewed.

Had he been able to do so, the newcomer would have observed a dapper-looking gentleman with receding grey hair, attired in a single-breasted suit with waistcoat, tie, and black, shiny shoes. The newcomer is, however, aware only of Pearson's voice. Journalist and author Richard King Huskinson, described by Pearson as 'one of our most devoted helpers', sets the scene:

A guide leads in the blinded soldier and he finds Sir Arthur [N.B. This was written retrospectively. Pearson was not in fact made baronet until July 1916] standing to welcome him; somehow or other, the hands of the two blind men meet. Sitting on the sofa, still holding the hand of his visitor, Sir Arthur begins at once to talk of the future.

No one can understand the power that one man has over another. If you were present at one of these interviews; if you attempted to analyse Sir Arthur's secret, you would probably say that he took it for granted that the blinded man was going to make a success of being blind. In a word, the man finds himself swept along by Sir Arthur's unfaltering convictions…. And you see the change in the man taking place, you hear a new tone in his voice—he has been carried over the dead point, and you realize that there will be no going back in his mind.

As for sympathy, it has been expressed by the touch of the hand resting on his, by Sir Arthur's genuine interest in his affairs. Eyes are not needed to catch the deep feeling under the brisk, confident tone in which everything has been said. The man knows that all is understood—this, more than anything else, makes a cheerful discussion of the future assuring. The sense of assurance is what, above all, is requisite. He finds himself laughing at difficulties, in better spirits, one would judge, than he had experienced since he was wounded. These interviews do not last very long, but they are very momentous, and he is an exceptional man who does not leave the room merely with a determination to make a success of his life, but with a new-found confidence that he can do so.[2]

For the newcomer to St Dunstan's there were practical difficulties to surmount—not least that of being able to find his way about. The corridors, said Pearson, were

covered with green carpet, with linoleum pathways running through it, and you will see upon the walls notices telling the visitors that they must keep off these pathways, which are only for the men, who hear each other approaching on them. These linoleum pathways have a great deal to do with the remarkable speed with which the men at St Dunstans get accustomed to moving about freely and easily.[3]

The men were advised to keep to the left, to avoid colliding with one another. 'As they walk along,' said Pearson, 'some of them sing out in a cheery voice to clear a way for themselves.'[4] In his book *The World is Mine* (published 1979), Australian Army Colonel (Joseph) Rex Hall said that sighted visitors found it 'difficult indeed to believe that [the residents] cannot see where they are going'.[5]

The top and bottom of each staircase was demarcated by a patch of rubber or wood set into the flooring, which the men's feet could instantly detect. Also, etched into the banisters were numbered notches, each corresponding with a particular step. In this way, having been told how many steps there were in total, the man was able to work out how many there were to go before he reached the top or bottom.

As for the dormitories, they were 'most comfortable; each fitted with standard furniture and carpeted'.[6] However, said Pearson, it was most important that every article of furniture should have its place and should not be moved without warning. A loud-ticking clock, a board that creaks, in winter the crackling of a fire in the grate, such things as these help a blinded man to walk about a room with confidence.[7]

As regards the outdoors, Pearson continued:

Passing through the house into the grounds you will find that there are boards let into the ground before steps and dangerous obstacles. These boards give warning through the feet of the blind men of the fact that they approaching danger.[8]

There were also ropes and handrails to guide them, with bosses set on top of their supporting wooden posts to signify junctions. These posts were padded with straw wound around with felt so that a man would not injure himself, should he happen to bump against them. However, Pearson stressed that whereas the handrails were very useful to newcomers, before long 'you will see them getting about quite well without any aid of the kind'.[9] Finally, each man was provided with a stout walking stick, although most St Dunstaners preferred not to use them.[10]

There were many other little tricks to be learned that would make life easier. For example, by the cupping of a finger over the lip of a glass, over-pouring could be avoided; lining up a cigarette end with the end of the match before striking, would ensure that the flame was in exactly the correct position to ignite the tip.

For those who wished to go walking or rowing on the nearby Regent's Park Lake, or to partake in physical drill, their day began at 6.30 a.m. Drill was usually conducted by a sighted ex-army non-commissioned officer, or occasionally by a St Dunstaner who could detect, by ear, when a man was not keeping good time with the others! Normally, however, the day commenced with breakfast taken at 8 a.m., after which a sighted person read aloud from the newspaper—news from the Front being of particular interest.[11]

Letters were delivered and read to the men by the VAD staff—described as 'wonderfully charming and attentive'.[12] The VADs became the companions of the blind men, who were able to describe to them what the various members of staff—themselves included—looked like. They described the weather; spring, for example, when late snows and frosts gave way to warming sunshine, bringing daffodils into flower and the trees of St Dunstan's beautiful grounds into leaf.

At 9.30 a.m. a whistle was blown for work to commence. From 12 a.m. the men were free to relax in the lounge, take a walk, or write letters until 1 p.m., when a bell was rung to signal lunchtime. At 2.30 p.m. the whistle was blown again and work recommenced until 4.30 p.m. From then on the men were left to their own devices. After supper, taken at 8 p.m., there were further newspaper readings for those who wished to avail themselves of this facility. Alternatively, a person might prefer to hear a story, read to him by one of the nursing staff. Finally, at 9.30 p.m. an orderly conducted the men to their various dormitories, and by 10 p.m. everyone was expected to be in bed.

Sometimes while promenading in the garden, the men would encounter Ruby Smith, born at St Dunstan's in 1912. She was the four-year-old daughter of the head gardener. Ruby, with her charm, friendliness, and exuberance, brought a new dimension to the lives of the blind men. Said she:

> I used to go up to them and chat, and we'd walk around just holding hands.... I used to ask them where they wanted to go. If they wanted to go to a certain workshop, I knew them all by heart. I knew where to find everything and I just used to paddle along with them. They were so pleased to have a child come and talk to them. I always remember how my little hand seemed so small in theirs.[13]

Ruby's weekly task was to bring the Chief a bouquet of roses, picked by her father.

Blinded soldier with little girl in red dress. Artist unknown. (*Blind Veterans UK*)

St Dunstan's Goes from Strength to Strength

A perusal of the minutes of the meetings of St Dunstan's Committee gives an interesting insight into the rapid evolution and expansion of that organization, which may be likened to a great orchestra, with Pearson as its conductor. To him fell the task of making sure that it functioned harmoniously, and that individuals—both St Dunstaners and staff—knew their responsibilities, and never failed to come in on cue. However, a problem he faced was how to keep St Dunstan's on a sound financial footing, while at the same time expanding its facilities and opening more annexes to cope with the increasing demand. It had become necessary, he said, 'to establish centres away from London where special cases could be treated, pleasant homes where men could be sent for periods of convalescence or for holidays'.[1] This he was able to achieve, thanks to his own abilities in the fields of publicity, organization, and fundraising; St Dunstan's benefited hugely from an immensely generous public, which was grateful to those who had given so much.

In April 1915, £1,000 of the £2,000 promised by the Committee of the Order of St John of Jerusalem and the British Red Cross Society was received.[2] On the 21st of that month the Committee resolved to seek Otto Kahn's permission for 'temporary wooden sleeping quarters' to be erected in the grounds of St Dunstan's. Also, 'the question of quarters for wives' of St Dunstaners was discussed, and it was decided that 'a suitable house as near to the hostel as possible' be hired for the purpose.[3]

On 30 April 1915, it was agreed that Arnold Lawson, Senior Ophthalmic Surgeon and Lecturer in Ophthalmic Surgery at London's Middlesex Hospital, would visit and attend to the blinded men of St Dunstan's, whereas Arthur W. Ormond of the Royal Army Medical Corps, Ophthalmic Surgeon at the 2nd London General Hospital, Chelsea, and also at London's Guy's Hospital, would have charge of the blinded men at St Mark's (i.e. at the 2nd London General Hospital).[4] On 3 May 1915, Ernest Kessell, Pearson's former secretary at Newnes' publishers, was appointed Treasurer.

On 17 May 1915, Pearson had much to report. Lady Beatty, wife of Admiral Beatty, Commander of the 1st Battlecruiser Squadron (and from 1916, Commander-in-Chief of the Grand Fleet), had offered to provide a wooden, single-storey, twenty-bedded dormitory to supplement the new sleeping quarters currently being constructed in the grounds. Also, the terrace was to be extended 'for dining and sleeping accommodation' and a new workshop was to be built. Two motor cars had been placed at the disposal of the hostel. A man was to be employed for duty at the gate, and another for duty in the hall on Saturday afternoons and Sundays.

Bedford College of Higher Education (for women), Regent's Park, founded in 1849, had offered 'to coach the men when doing morning exercise', and the manager of the Queens Theatre promised to donate the entire proceeds of a performance to be given on 24 June to St Dunstan's. A tenancy agreement for 124 Regent's Park Road was also signed. This was for the use of the wives and friends of St Dunstaners.

Finally, having learnt of the work of the Paris branch of the Red Cross Society, Pearson promised to 'make it his business to keep in touch with those in Paris,' and 'forward them a report of the work here'.[5] On 28 May 1915, a comparison was made between the two:

> Dr Leon P. Comein, attached to the Belgian Army had paid a visit to St Dunstan's and declared that the work being done there was far in advance of that in Paris.

There were thirty St Dunstaners in residence, of whom three were Belgian and two were officers—both Irishmen. Pearson regarded St Dunstan's in Regent's Park as being the perfect environment for the rehabilitation of his men:[6]

> No sound is [heard] here of the London traffic. The rustle of the breeze in the foliage is creative to the blind man—making the trees stand out clearly to his mental vision.[7]

In June 1915 the Committee felt it 'necessary at the earliest possible date to obtain separate quarters for blinded officers'. An offer of assistance was received from the International Correspondence School (US organization for distance learning). 124 Regent's Park Road was now fully operational. Meanwhile, two committee members, Mr Tindal Robertson and Miss Austin, had paid a visit to the training home for blinded soldiers in Paris.[8]

In July 1915 the Countess of Gosford, President of the Central Workrooms of the British Red Cross Society, joined the Committee. Sir John Stirling Maxwell of Keir, 10th Baronet, and his wife Lady Ann placed their house, 'No. 21 Portland Place, at the disposal of the Committee till six months after the War'. The problem of where to accommodate the St Dunstaner officers was thereby solved.[9]

In September 1915, Lady Beatty donated £498 17s 3d towards the cost of the new buildings and the sum of £105 was received from the New Zealand Government. In the same month Pearson explained to the Committee that 'hostile air raids had made the conservatory a very undesirable place as sleeping quarters for the men. He proposed that a new building for the purpose should be erected on the Terrace.'

It was agreed that 'teaching arrangements' were to be transferred to Great Portland Street. Miss V. Brown was engaged as teacher of Braille; Mrs Brighurst as assistant massage teacher;[10] and Mr Thomas H. Martin, 'to undertake the work of settling in their occupations the men who leave St Dunstan's,' with Mr H. Clayden as his assistant. In September, twelve more men were ready to leave the hostel, having 'graduated' from St Dunstan's.[11] The next month Pearson reported that a number of the men were 'anxious to learn Braille-shorthand and others wished to become divers. There were openings for men qualified in both these subjects.' In March 1916, St Dunstaner Thomas P. Drummond, an Australian Sapper in the Royal Naval Division (Engineers) who had been blinded at the Dardanelles in May 1915, commenced his tuition as a maritime diver.[12] Thanks to St Dunstan's he duly qualified as a diver, and worked for a short time for a salvage company. However, it was discovered that several others were required to supervise the blind diver and this was uneconomical for the employer. Drummond retrained as a masseur before returning to Australia. Although popular, the occupation of maritime diver was subsequently deemed to be unsuitable for St Dunstan's graduates.

Further support for St Dunstan's came from Dr William M. Mollison, aurist to Guy's Hospital, who volunteered to treat any St Dunstaners with ear conditions.[13] Then, in November 1915, St Dunstan's was again honoured by royal endorsement as Queen Alexandra, the Queen Mother (and widow of the late King Edward VII who died in 1910), Princess Victoria, and the Duchess George of Russia paid a visit to St Dunstan's. According to Pearson, they were 'greatly pleased to note the way in which matters were proceeding'.

A further nine St Dunstaners had 'graduated' by November, followed by eight more the next month; the new school building had been completed and was now operational, and the NIB would henceforth assume responsibility for the aftercare of St Dunstaner's.[14] In December the new typing-room adjacent to the Braille room was completed. St Dunstan's closed for the Christmas holidays for a period of about ten days and the men returned to their homes.[15]

By the end of 1915, St Dunstan's had spread well beyond Regent's Park. An annexe at Brighton in a house in Queen's Road, lent by the NIB, served as a convalescent home for men just discharged from hospital and for others who needed a change or a rest. Another annexe, opened in Torquay 'with local financial support', was 'for those in need of longer convalescence—for those who had lost limbs as well as sight, for the shell shocked and paralysed, the more sorely hurt in body and mind'.

In January 1916, Pearson reported that a sum in excess of £9,000 in subscriptions had been received since the last Committee meeting. Also, an agreement had been made 'for the occupation for one or two terms of Townsend House, St John's Wood, which would be used for sleeping purposes only'. There had been eight more graduations, Queen Alexandra had again visited St Dunstan's, and also Lord Kitchener.[16]

In February 1916 there were further acts of generosity to report: an offer by Hamilton Edwards of Basingstoke of five plots of land 'for the purpose of assisting Blinded Soldiers to take up poultry farming', and a collection organized by Mr Kenneth Bilbrough which raised the sum of £6,000 for the hostel. Despite all the support, Pearson feared that, with the increasing numbers of returning war-blinded men, the accommodation on offer seemed 'likely to prove insufficient for requirements'. In other words, the hostel was continually finding itself having to play 'catch up'.

St Dunstan's' first Annual Report for the year ending 26 March 1916 contained good tidings. Queen Alexandra had 'graciously signified her desire to become Patroness' of the organization.[17] From henceforth, she would make frequent visits to St Dunstan's, often informally. There were now 150 St Dunstaners in residence.

In April 1916, Pearson announced that he had succeeded in finding suitable accommodation for twenty-six St Dunstaner trainee masseurs at 12 Sussex Place. Mr A. D. Hall of the East London Workshops for the Blind was to be employed to supervise the work of those men who had completed their training. Mr Charles E. Rose, Superintendent of the Workshops, was invited to join the Committee,[18] as was Sir Benjamin Franklin, the Surgeon General.

Pearson's concerns regarding funding were eased significantly when wealthy philanthropist Mrs Agnes Marke Wood donated £5,000 'for the permanent Aftercare Fund',[19] and in May the Committee of the National Relief Fund agreed 'to grant a further fifteen thousand pounds to be devoted to the ordinary current expenses of St Dunstan's'. It was proposed that in addition to the present allowance of 2s 6d for each child of a married St Dunstaner, a further 2s 6d per week was to be granted by the Committee.[20]

Miss J. E. Davidson resigned as Matron in May and the next month Dr C. Chittenden Bridges was appointed St Dunstan's' regular medical officer.

By June 1916, eight men (having passed the necessary examination) had become qualified masseurs. Of these, four had obtained appointments in a military hospital in Manchester, and two at the 3rd London General Hospital, while the remaining two—a Canadian and New Zealander—were to return to their respective countries.

In July 1916, while the hostel was closed for a month's summer holiday,[21] Pearson was awarded a baronetcy for his services to the blind. He took the title 1st Baronet of St Dunstan's. In that year, he relinquished his interest in the *Daily Express* newspaper—the ownership of which passed to Max Aitken.

In August 1916, Miss Frances Hughes was appointed the new Matron. As she was from Ireland, she became known to the men as 'Sister Pat'. Said she:

> I must say my first thoughts on coming to St Dunstan's were that it would be a very sad post for me; but since being here I find you all so 'merry and bright' and cheery at work and play, that it is proving the jolliest job I ever had.[22]

In September 1916, Miss Irene Mace, a VAD and Pearson's personal assistant and guide, joined the Committee. Pearson reported that it was necessary to erect yet more new buildings 'for the proper accommodation of the men', and work was begun to this end.[23]

In October 1916, Pearson approached the Reverend Dr Pearce Gould with regard to Holford House, a large mansion adjacent to St Dunstan's and the home of Regent's Park College, to ask if it could be used as a temporary annexe. Gould was Principal of the College which offered degrees in law and the arts, and also training in the Christian ministry; he agreed to Pearson's request and accommodation was thereby provided for an extra 200 men, making an enormous difference to St Dunstan's ability to cope with the demands currently being made upon it. Meanwhile, 'the work of building a new lounge on the lawn was well in hand'.

The NIB offered St Dunstan's the use of West House, 12–14 Portland Place, Kemp Town, Brighton. This would provide accommodation for sixty men and 'serve very well as a rest home for some of the men who required a change'. It was also suggested that the Matron of St Dunstan's 'should be given the rank of Commandant'.[24]

In November 1916 a further sum of £20,000 was granted to St Dunstan's by the National Relief Fund. Miss Margaret Power, 'a very capable lady and a trained nurse', was appointed Matron to the new College Annexe at Holford House. A house at Lee Terrace, Blackheath, was placed at the disposal of the Committee (free of charge) and had been fitted up as an annexe

Left to right: St Dunstan's; Bungalow Annex; College Annexe. (*Blind Veterans UK*)

'where men requiring a rest and change would be sent'. Finally, Pearson reported that 'various additional buildings to St Dunstan's, including the Chapel' are 'proceeding satisfactorily'.[25]

In December 1916, at the request of the King, Pearson crossed the Channel to France to inspect 'a number of the comparatively small and scattered institutions at which the blinded French soldiers were being trained'.[26] Pearson subsequently remarked that St Dunstan's 'had the pleasure of welcoming' a French officer and three French private soldiers whom he had met during his visit to France 'and who had evinced a particular desire to make a stay with us'.[27] Therefore, in addition to providing training to blinded servicemen from Britain and the Empire, Pearson had even managed to 'poach' some Frenchmen!

Other notable visitors who came to boost the morale of the blinded men in that year of 1916 were the explorer Sir Ernest Shackleton and Queen Amelie of Portugal. The latter made a tour of the workshops and talked freely with the men, not realizing that when they were at work, such a practice was actively discouraged by the powers that be!

In January 1917, Pearson informed the Committee that the new annexe at Titchfield Terrace, St John's Wood, was 'working satisfactorily'. He also confirmed the purchase by the NIB of two houses at Brighton, to be used as convalescent annexes by the men of St Dunstan's.[28] Six months later, on 7 June 1917, Pearson announced that the workshops were completed and occupied.

> Extensions to the Braille and typewriting rooms were proceeding satisfactorily and… it was hoped the new [so-called 'Bungalow'] annexe would be ready for occupation on the 25th June.

On the subject of the teaching of Braille, Pearson took a relaxed attitude. It was his view that 'those men not really wishing to learn and who could not benefit to any great extent by learning, [should be] allowed to forego this part of the training at St Dunstan's'. Meanwhile,

Sir Ernest Shackleton
and Sir Arthur Pearson
at St Dunstan's. (*Blind
Veterans UK*)

a poultry farm at Kings Langley had been acquired by the NIB to enable the men learning poultry farming at St Dunstan's to obtain more practical experience.

In March the National Relief Fund agreed to provide a further £15,000 towards the construction of the new buildings. By April the Committee had changed somewhat: Sir Benjamin Franklin had died, and Lady Gosford, the Hon. Arthur Stanley and Mr P. Tindal Robertson had resigned their posts.[29] The appointments of sighted overseers in the workshops were approved; Mrs Craven was appointed Under-Matron and Captain Roberts, Adjutant, while Captain Ward was appointed Adjutant to the new annexe.[30]

After a visit to the hostel by Colonel Guy L. Foster, Canadian Director of Medical Services to St Dunstan's, Pearson reported that in future 'every Canadian blinded soldier shall, before being allowed to return to Canada, be given an opportunity of entering St Dunstan's'.[31]

By 24 July 1917 the Bungalow Annexe was 'in full swing' with thirty-five residents. Since the last Committee meeting, nine St Dunstaners had 'passed the examinations of the Incorporated Society of Trained Masseuses & that for all, satisfactory and remunerative posts at Military Hospitals had been secured'.[32]

Types of Eye Injury and their Treatment

We came upon him sitting in the sun,
Blinded by war, and left. And past the fence
There came young soldiers from the Hand and Flower,
Asking advice of his experience.

And he said this, and that, and told them tales,
And all the nightmares of each empty head
Blew into air; then, hearing us beside,
'Poor chaps, how'd they know what it's like?' he said.

And we stood there, and watched him as he sat,
Turning his sockets where they went away,
Until it came to one of us to ask
'And you're—how old?'
'Nineteen, the third of May.'

The Veteran by Margaret Postgate Cole

Pearson was unstinting in his praise for 'the distinguished specialists in almost every branch of the medical profession who freely placed their invaluable services at our disposal.'[1] They included the 'eminent voluntary oculists and the doctor' who visited daily to attend to the men's eyes, and also to those on the sick list and to those who had become more seriously ill and 'were cared for in our own little private hospital'. The 'eminent oculists', referred to above, were the aforementioned Arthur W. Ormond and Arnold Lawson.

During the period 1914–19 no less than 1,008 blinded men came under the care of Arthur W. Ormond as in-patients at the 2nd London General Hospital (and another 11,081 were treated as out-patients).[2]

All these men, with one or two exceptions, were transferred to St Dunstan's for training, after their wounds had healed sufficiently to allow them to leave the hospital.[3]

Sir Arnold Lawson's book (in 1920 he received a knighthood), published in 1922 and entitled *War Blindness at St Dunstan's*, is an account of the medical (ophthalmic) work which he

Sir Arnold Lawson.
(*Royal College of Ophthalmologists*)

performed at that institution from 1915–20. It includes details of the men who lost their sight, either completely, or to the extent that only a small amount of useful vision remained, and of the circumstances in which this came about. As for Pearson, Lawson described him as 'a man … endowed with great intellectual capacity and marvellous powers of organization.' His greatest achievement, said Lawson, was to realize 'that it was still possible for him to carry on after his loss [of sight] as well and in some ways better than he had done before.'[4]

Causes of Blindness

A study of *War Blindness at St Dunstan's* led to a remarkable conclusion: 417 out of the total of 825 patients who came under Lawson's care during the wartime period had lost their sight for reasons *other than* those directly connected with their wartime service—in other words, through accident and disease. Of these 417 cases of so-called 'Non- traumatic Blindness', no less than 127 had become blind from being infected with the venereal disease syphilis, which has the capacity to damage not only the eye, but also the optic nerve and even the brain itself. In fact, 33 of these men were suffering from *tabes dorsalis*—an advanced stage of syphilis in which the spinal cord is affected. Another appalling legacy of syphilis is that, in its final stages, it renders the sufferer insane. It was for this reason that some St Dunstaners ended their days in psychiatric hospitals. Poignantly, Lawson cited the cases of five St Dunstaner 'lads' aged twenty, twenty-one, twenty-two, twenty-two, and twenty-five respectively, all of whom were already quite blind from syphilitic infection. How had they become infected? Clearly these men, many of whom were little more than boys, and away from their homes and families, wives and girlfriends for the very first time, had sought solace in the arms of Belgian and French prostitutes. Sadly, in those days, no antibiotics were available with which to treat them.

Other causes of non-traumatic blindness were the presence of a tumour within the brain and cerebro-spinal meningitis. There were also eleven cases of glaucoma—the very same disease which had caused Pearson himself to become blind. Those whose blindness was directly attributable to traumatic injury—the so-called 'Traumatic Blindness' category—numbered 408, and Lawson again subdivided these according to cause. Here, it should be remembered that for a person to be able to see, the whole of the visual pathway (i.e. from the retina of the eye to the visual cortex, and from there to regions of the brain which are concerned with interpretation of shapes, moving objects and so forth) must be intact. Seventy-two had suffered bullet wounds to the orbits (the bony sockets in which the eyeballs rest); seventeen had suffered fractures of the back (occipital region) of the skull (the left and right occipital lobes of the brain contain the main centre for the processing of visual information—the so-called visual cortex); twelve had been blinded as a result of fractures of bones adjacent to the apex (rear) of the orbits and the optic canals (through which the optic nerves travel); and sixteen had experienced concussion (being rendered unconscious) from the explosion of a shell or bomb, the blast having been of such severity as to damage the brain irreparably.

Of the 289 'Miscellaneous Cases' in the 'Traumatic Blindness' category, all had been blinded by 'direct smashing injuries from in front, or by perforation of the globes [eyeballs] by fragments of metal or other flying bodies'.[5] In only two of these cases was blindness caused by bayonet wounds.

Ormond differentiated between injuries to the eye caused by contusion on the one hand, and concussion on the other. Contusion blindness results from the direct physical impact of bullet, shrapnel, or blow. Concussion blindness is caused by violent shaking, say, from the blast of an explosion, leading to tissue damage to, or haemorrhage inside the eye itself.

> One of the principal features of the War was the number of cases of functional blindness [i.e. blindness which had no discernible organic cause] due to the violent explosions caused by high explosive shells, bombs, hand-grenades, &c. Usually the patient had been rendered unconscious by an explosion in his close vicinity, and on regaining consciousness he found that he was unable to see.

The curious feature of such patients, said Ormond, was that although they 'were undoubtedly psychically [i.e. inexplicably] blind… [their] pupils reacted normally and the fundus showed no definite changes'. This suggests that the cause of blindness in such patients was damage not to the eyes themselves, but to those parts of the brain associated with sight.[6]

Some St Dunstaners had been blinded in the most extraordinary ways. One was using a detonator as a pencil case, believing it to be empty. When he rammed a pencil into it with particular force, it exploded, blinding him in both eyes. Another was using a 16-inch metal file as a cricket bat when it flew out of its handle, perforating his left eye and fracturing the right orbit. The right eye had to be removed and the left remained permanently blind through damage to the tissues behind the eyeball. In another case, when a company had taken over a building from the enemy, a man was ordered by his sergeant to chop up some wood which was lying in a corner. As he was chopping, the wood exploded. The timber had apparently been hollowed out and an egg-bomb placed inside. (This latter event had occurred only two days before the signing of the Armistice.) In another incident a man tripped when attempting to force his way through a barbed-wire entanglement. In his fall, his left eye was pierced by the barbed wire, which also damaged the cornea of his right eye. The left eye had to be removed.

A number of pilots serving in the Royal Flying Corps were also blinded. A nineteen-year-old pilot collided with another aircraft whilst taxiing and experienced a severe blow to the upper part of his face. Although the eyes showed no signs of external injury, both retinas were severely damaged. Another pilot was shot down; whereupon his aircraft caught fire. Although he was extricated from it, he was 'horribly burnt all over his face, arms, and body'. As for his eyes, there was very severe corneal ulceration which almost destroyed the sight in one eye. In the other, there was 'a large, bulging corneal scar with adherent iris' and raised intra-ocular pressure. Lawson, therefore, performed an iridectomy (surgical removal of part of the iris) thereby successfully reducing the pressure and enabling the man to retain sufficient sight for him 'to see about the room and recognize large objects fairly close to him'. Sadly, he died a year or so later.[7]

Gas and Blindness

Gas was used for the first time as a weapon of war in August 1914 by the French in the form of tear-gas grenades containing xylyl bromide. This was contrary to the terms of the Hague Convention, which expressly forbade the use of 'poison or poisoned weapons'.[8] However, this substance is more of an irritant than something that can kill.

The first major use of poison gas occurred at the 2nd Battle of Ypres on 22 April 1915 when the German Pioneer Regiment No. 35 deployed chlorine against French positions near Boezinge, situated to the north of Ypres in the Ypres Salient. As its density is approximately 2.5 times greater than that of air, chlorine gas, when released, will initially remain close to the ground, provided that there is little air movement. It was therefore an ideal substance to be floated across no man's land towards an enemy trench, into which it sank.

The men had no gas masks (the 'box respirator'—a mask, attached to a filter—was not issued until late in 1916), and the only counter-measure was for the soldier to soak his handkerchief or puttees in water or urine and clap it over his face—something which there was hardly time or opportunity to do in the heat of battle. Eyes are seldom damaged severely by chlorine gas, although temporary blindness resulted sometimes. However, burns to the cornea could lead to corneal ulceration, and subsequent scarring and opacity.

The Germans went on to produce more lethal varieties of gas, including phosgene in December 1915 and mustard gas in mid-1917. Phosgene is highly toxic, irritating, and corrosive. If it comes into contact with the eye, it reacts slowly with moisture therein to produce hydrochloric acid. Mustard gas (so-called because of its aroma) had the ability to penetrate clothing and every type of gas mask then in service. It causes irritation of the eyes, swelling of the eyelids, and sensitivity to light. Vision is lost as the cornea becomes ulcerated and then decays. It also causes blisters to form on the skin, which may turn gangrenous.

A harrowing image of the First World War is that of soldiers who have been the victims of a gas attack. They walk slowly in procession, each with a hand on the shoulder of the one in front, as they are guided by a sighted person to the regimental first-aid post. This scene was immortalized by US painter John Singer Sargent in his painting 'Gassed'.

In view of the widespread use in the First World War of increasingly toxic forms of poison

'Gassed' by John Singer Sargent, August 1918. (*IWM*)

gas, it might be supposed that St Dunstan's would be inundated with the victims of gas-induced eye injuries. This was not the case; if the damage was severe enough to blind, then it was usually severe enough to kill, usually from damage to the lungs from the effects of inhalation. However, Ormond did describe two men in whom gas had caused 'such severe injuries to the cornea that complete opacity of each resulted'. Both men were subsequently transferred to St Dunstan's.[9]

The *Saint Dunstan's Annual*, published in 1935, contained a disturbing article, stating that even seventeen years after the end of the First World War, men were continuing to lose their sight as a result of having been gassed almost two decades previously in 1917 or 1918. This included five new cases in the previous twelve months alone. There was no doubt that the culprit was not lachrymatory gases (such as tear gas) or chlorine, but mustard gas.[10]

Treatment

Ormond described how it was possible to remove metal fragments from the eye by the use of an electro-magnet. However, he confessed that 'the results of the extraction of foreign bodies' by this method 'when they have penetrated deeply into the globe are disappointing.'[11]

Although urgent medical treatment, including surgery, was given both in the theatre of war and subsequently in dedicated UK hospitals, such as the 2nd London General Hospital, Chelsea, there were several conditions which presented ongoing problems:

Interstitial keratitis—a condition in which blood vessels grow into the cornea and render it opaque. It may be the result of a traumatic injury to the cornea, or of an infection such as syphilis. It was treated by iridectomy which was believed to improve the nutrition of the eye.

Retinal detachment—treated by scleral trephining, whereby a small incision was made into the white of the eye (sclera) in order to reduce the pressure within.

Glaucoma—also treated by scleral trephining and iridectomy; the object again being to reduce the pressure in the eyes which would otherwise destroy the optic nerve. (This was the same operation which Pearson himself had undergone, but without success.)

Traumatic cataract (opacity of the lens due to trauma)—in mild cases, a 'cataract lens' (hand-held magnifying glass) was prescribed to improve the vision. However, if the cataract was so dense that it seriously impeded the vision, then, with the patient's consent, it was surgically removed. Ormond described 'the happiest experience… of the men who had traumatic cataracts, who by their subsequent needling and evacuation of the lens material, got reading vision with proper glasses. If (and there have been about twenty such cases) vision after the removal of the lens gave them 6/18 or better with correction, they were not kept at St Dunstan's.'[12] (In needling, a 'needle knife' is inserted into the periphery of the cornea, and used to lever the opaque lens away from its supporting tissue. The lens is then removed. However, the eye is now unable to focus, and therefore spectacles are required.)

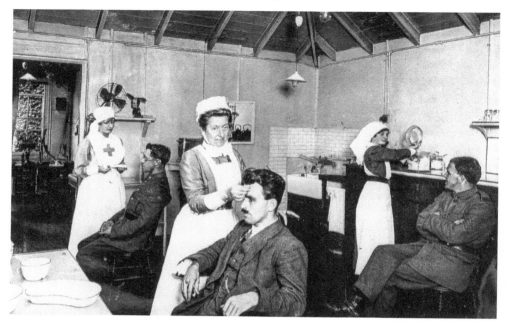

The Dispensary. (*Blind Veterans UK*)

Inflamed, or discharging eyes and eye sockets—frequent bathing and irrigation was required at one of St Dunstan's' two dispensaries.

Although a number of St Dunstaners possessed corneas which Lawson described as 'hazy', he made no mention of ever having performed a corneal graft. Evidently, this was not common practice in those days—even though the first corneal graft was performed as early as 1905 by the Viennese ophthalmologist Eduard Zirm. However, as regards corneal ulcers, usually caused by traumatic injury, Ormond declared that 'the result of the treatment of these cases [was] very satisfactory'.[13]

Artificial, or 'glass', eyes were prescribed to fill empty sockets. However, those men who disliked the idea of wearing them were at liberty to request that Lawson close the eyelids of the affected eye permanently, with sutures.

Some men who were only temporarily blinded joined St Dunstan's briefly, but left when their sight returned. Sadly, however, for the vast majority admitted between 1914 and 1918, it proved impossible to save their sight. The same was true of the majority of those who were admitted subsequently, suffering from the long-term effects on their eyes of injuries or illnesses. For as Lawson said, 'no matter how quiet the eyes, or how long a time the disease has been stationary, old inflammatory mischief is always apt to recrudesce under conditions inimical to general health'.[14] However, even if only a slight improvement was obtained, it was a comfort to the men to know that they were to be attended to on an ongoing basis by two of the finest ophthalmologists in London. It should also be mentioned that in addition to the medical and ophthalmic specialists, there was a 'great army of men and women' who helped Pearson in his work, 'the majority of them giving up their time without any payment whatever'.[15]

Pearson's Brainchild in Operation

The Bishop tells us: 'When the boys come back
They will not be the same; for they'll have fought
In a just cause: they lead the last attack

On Anti-Christ; their comrades' blood has bought
New right to breed an honourable race,
They have challenged Death and dared him face to face.'

'We're none of us the same!' the boys reply.

For George lost both his legs; and Bill's stone blind;
Poor Jim's shot through the lungs and like to die;
And Bert's gone syphilitic: you'll not find

A chap who's served that hasn't found *some* change.'
And the Bishop said: 'The ways of God are strange!'

'They' by Siegfried Sassoon, 31 October 1916

Medical Care

The most seriously injured of those admitted to St Dunstan's were sent to the Torquay Annexe for convalescence. Its staff included a medical officer and doctor, a matron, fully-trained nursing staff, and a chaplain. Otherwise, those who required operative treatment were sent either to St Dunstan's Hospital in Sussex Place, London, or to one of the London hospitals. If required, St Dunstan's would then arrange for a period of convalescence at one of its annexes.

For the amputee, artificial limbs were provided, and in the case of those who had lost one or both arms, a series of experiments were commenced to discover which type of prosthesis was best suited to their needs. Every effort was made to accommodate such men, even to the extent of races being organized for one-armed oarsmen on nearby Regent's Park Lake.

Braille classroom. (*Blind Veterans UK*)

Tuition

'Very quickly', said Pearson, 'I realized that it is the blind man who, above all, needs occupation, and that the more active, the more normal he can make his life, the happier he will be.'[1] He acknowledged, however, that some men were unable to work, either because of severe physical injury or mental trauma. In this case, St Dunstan's would provide accommodation for them at one of its convalescent annexes. St Dunstaner Ian Fraser said that happily there were very few such men because Pearson 'succeeded in inspiring almost anyone who could work, with the desire to work'.[2]

Although he did not want to force the learning of Braille on St Dunstaners, having worked for the NIB, Pearson was highly enthusiastic about the subject; he wanted to teach this skill to as many St Dunstaners as possible. This would, of course, be impossible for those who had lost hands, or whose hands were seriously injured.

Braille was taught in the following way. During their first lesson,

[The men were each provided] with a board having six small holes in two vertical rows, the holes [being] numbered to 6, then they were given pins with letters of the alphabet, which were manipulated until they memorized how to relate the pins to the holes, and so on until they mastered the whole alphabet.[3]

(The letters demarcating the holes, and those on the pins, were presumably embossed.) While

Typewriting classroom. (*Blind Veterans UK*)

acknowledging that Braille was a difficult skill to master, Pearson declared that for a blind man, there was

> a special delight in being able to read to himself, above all because in this way is provided a resource which enables him to fill in any unoccupied time when he happens to be alone. It gives him entrance to the world of books and brings back to him some of the independence he has lost. Not only books, but monthly magazines and weekly newspapers are produced in Braille—and between blind people correspondence by this medium is carried on without the need of relying on a sighted person to read aloud the letters received. To be able to write in Braille is a great advantage in that it enables a blind man to record and read his own notes and attend personally to his private business papers. Many of the soldiers who are now poultry-farmers and tradesmen keep their accounts in Braille with complete success.[4]

As an incentive, every man who passed the Braille reading test was, on leaving St Dunstan's, presented with a Braille writing machine. Furthermore, those who passed the Braille writing test (which was much more difficult) were presented with a gold watch-chain.[5] Said Pearson:

> The handwriting of a blinded man deteriorates inevitably and more or less rapidly, and therefore every blinded soldier learns to typewrite, not as a business, but simply to aid him the more quickly to recover from the effects of that loss of independence which is as serious a result as the loss of sight.

Masseurs in training. (*Blind Veterans UK*)

For a blind man to typewrite is much easier than you might think. Our men use ordinary machines. There is no difference in the keyboard, but the scale is in Braille characters.[6]

For typing training, the instructor was a sighted person, and the time [taken] to gain proficiency was from three to six months, according to the time available to the trainees to practise.[7] Finally, having passed the typewriting test, each man was presented with a 'Remington' typewriter of his own.

As regards shorthand typing, Pearson said,

By means of an adaptation of the Braille system, and a very ingenious little machine, our blinded soldiers leave St Dunstans absolutely guaranteed to write shorthand at a minimum speed of one hundred words a minute.[8]

Telephony was a popular subject, and more than 100 St Dunstaners became telephonists— many going on to spend their entire career with one company.[9]

Massage (or physiotherapy, as it is called today) was also popular, and there was a great demand by hospitals all over the country for qualified masseurs. On the lighter side, the preliminary course of massage instruction offered by St Dunstan's provided excellent opportunities for jokes and pranks, as, for example, when a trainee masseur placed a skeleton (used to demonstrate practical anatomy), complete with bowler hat, scarf and pipe, at the front door of the physiotherapy classroom. This was just before Pearson was due to arrive to show a distinguished visitor around!

Captain Francis P. Peirson-Webber in the 1920s.
(*Margaret Berryman*)

Trainees subsequently underwent an advanced training course at the NIB in Great Portland Street, London, at the end of which they sat for the (difficult) examination of the Incorporated Society of Trained Masseurs. This was followed by a year of additional training in a military hospital.

Poultry farming was popular with St Dunstaners—both those from Britain and from the Empire—some of whom had worked on farms before they were blinded. Their mentor was Captain Francis P. Peirson-Webber.

In 1899, Peirson-Webber was thrown from his horse while serving as Chief Staff Officer to the Pochi Field Force on India's North-West Frontier. He was rendered unconscious for some time, and was laid down face up to the sun; the strength of the light permanently blinded him. Thereafter, he was always most particular to refer to himself as 'blinded', and he would correct anyone who referred to him as 'blind'.[10] On his return to England, Peirson-Webber was eager to find an occupation for himself:

[He] shuddered at the idea of continued inertness, and after learning the usual accomplishments of the blind, he took a diploma in poultry husbandry and subsequently took a farm at Stockton in Warwickshire.

'My blindness does not stop me from judging poultry. I get hold of them, and from the feel of the feathers, the shape of the head and beak, the size and shape of the spurs, and the general conformation of the body, I can tell within a little time the breed of the bird, its condition, its age and other particulars.'

In 1906, he founded and became Director of the National Poultry Club.[11]

Above: Poultry farming.
(*Sport and General*)

Left: Breeding rabbits.
(*Blind Veterans UK*)

Cobblers' workshop. (*Blind Veterans UK*)

At Pearson's request, Captain Peirson-Webber came to St Dunstan's and started a poultry class. He had sighted instructors to help him. St Dunstaner Ian Fraser describes the class:

[Pupils also] learnt rough carpentry, so that they could make things like hen-coops, sitting boxes, and gates.[12]

Our Country Life Section, initiated by Captain [Peirson-] Webber and sighted assistants, gave instructions in two courses, each of six weeks. There were examinations, oral and practical, at the end of each course. The training was very thorough, and included subjects like the prevention and cure of poultry diseases. The men were also taught about ducks and turkeys, and even rabbit-breeding; and there was some simple market gardening—mostly growing vegetables and foods for the birds. The last month of training was done on a real poultry-farm: first at Dollis Hill, Finchley and then at King's Langley in Hertfordshire, where we set up a farm of our own. Each man could bring his wife or other relatives who were going to help him, so that they could learn their part of the work under sighted supervision.[13]

Once a man had been trained, said Pearson, 'he knows how to run an incubator and foster mother, and how to truss and prepare a bird for table so that it can be placed right in the window of a poulterer's shop.'[14]

The most popular of all the trades taught at St Dunstan's was boot-repairing or 'snobbing', as the men nicknamed it. The course—eight months in duration—was combined with mat-

Joinery. (*Blind Veterans UK*)

making, and for good reason; out in the workplace, there may be twenty pairs of boots to repair one week and only half a dozen the next. In a slack week the man can make a few mats and have the advantage of a change of work.[15]

Pearson described a typical scene in the workshop:

A very large number of men are busy here—it is a scene of intense, orderly activity and movement; and on all sides you will hear men whistling or singing as they work. The Cobblers' Chorus, accompanied by blows of hammer upon leather sole, is a never-ending source of wonder and delight to the visitor.[16]

He went on to say how careful the novice boot-repairer was to affix his first sole to the shell of the boot, and then shape and finish it, using leather of the best quality, supplied to him by St Dunstan's, and how the skilled instructor 'permitted nothing to pass that was not first-rate'.[17]

Visitors were fascinated to watch as the blind man put a handful of tingles (fine nails) into his mouth, then pushed them forward, one at a time, and held them between his lips, ready to be taken and used. There was an ingeniously designed punch by which holes could be made at intervals around the perimeter of the sole. Then, all he had to do was feel for these holes to determine exactly where each tingle should go.

When they had achieved a degree of proficiency, the men were entrusted to repair the footwear of the local people of St John's Wood, who were only too willing to show an interest and support the cause. Also, four or five pairs of army boots per week were taken in to be repaired.

Carpentry and joinery were so much enjoyed by the men that few of them downed tools when the whistle blew at 4.30 p.m. Sometimes they continued with their making of cabinets, picture frames, dog kennels, etc. until well into the evening: 'visitors were sometimes startled to hear the sounds of hammering and sawing executed with confidence coming from a completely dark workshop'.[18]

It was found, said Pearson, that in respect of carpentry, there was more profit in the production of smaller objects such as 'ornamental tables, tea-trays, photo frames and the like' than there was in the manufacture of large objects such as wardrobes and dining room tables.[19]

St Dunstan's was famous for its production of string bags, which were traditionally knitted on a circular, wooden frame, with pegs spaced at 1-inch intervals around its perimeter. Finally, two lengths of string were plaited to make the handles. There was friendly rivalry among the men as to who could knit a string bag in the shortest time, the winner earning the title 'The Bag King'! Tennis nets and netting for hammocks and fruit cages were also made.

Motivation

Ian Fraser issued a caveat; there were some men who even the expert and enthusiastic staff of St Dunstan's could not succeed in motivating. Furthermore, Consultant Ophthalmologist Arnold Lawson pointed out that in respect of work, motivating the blinded officers sometimes proved more difficult than motivating the other ranks. This was because the officers, more often than not, had sufficient means to opt out of working. The non-commissioned men, on the other hand, were obliged to augment their pensions by every means in their power.[20]

Leisure

It was generally acknowledged that the men of St Dunstan's learned more quickly than those at other institutions for the blind; the reason, said Pearson, was that their lives did not consist of all work and no play. 'Exercise', he said, 'improves the mind just as it improves the muscles.[21] The men are put to play before they can feel brain-fag and mental strain.'[22] In accordance with this philosophy, Pearson introduced a number of activities into the curriculum:

[These] were designed, not merely to bring gaiety to the lives of the blinded men, but to draw out their powers of enjoyment. To instruct them in practical accomplishments was a very important part of our work, but it was not everything. My plan went far beyond that. Indeed it seemed to me that the blinded man required more encouragement in the direction of play than in that of work.[23]

Outdoor pastimes were encouraged, such as tandem-cycling, swimming, walking, running, sack races, and physical drill. Visitors to Regent's Park, said Pearson, might see in the distance,

a curious white caterpillar winding its way over the green grass. This is twenty or thirty men in their white sweaters and shorts jogging on their way down to the lake—each man with his hand on the shoulder of the man in advance of his, and the man who can see in the lead.[24]

Tug-of-war. (*Blind Veterans UK*)

Rowing on Regent's Park Lake, summer 1918. (*Blind Veterans UK*)

Dancing Class, 1918. (*Blind Veterans UK*)

For the youngsters, boxing and wrestling matches were held regularly in the gymnasium. Pearson enthused about how the men took to rowing on nearby Regent's Park Lake, with ladies from nearby Bedford College acting as coxwains. Sidney Dark sets the scene:

> In the summertime a whole army of girls regularly got up early in the morning to steer the St Dunstan's boats for an hour or two before going on to their shops and offices.
> Any summer morning in the years of the war there might be seen on the Regent's Park Lake two or three hundred young men in shorts and sweaters full of eager life, looking forward to the future with the courage and the certainty that should characterize youth—all of them blind, and all of them a few months before, despondent, hopeless, broken.[25]

Displaying a degree of ruthlessness, Pearson declared,

> The Regent's Park Lake runs into our grounds and we have settled the question as to who shall use it by simply hiring all of the boats. Three times a day that lake is full of blind oarsmen, and numbers of the men who have never handled an oar before have become quite proficient.[26]

'To the blinded man,' he said, 'there is joy in being out on the water, pleasure in the exercise, pleasure in handling the oars, pleasure in the sense of movement, pleasure in the sounds that are full of pictorial suggestion.'[27] As for Pearson himself, a particular pleasure was to gallop his horse 'fearlessly over the Downs,' even when he had lost his sight completely.[28] He was also an enthusiastic dancer. 'Dancing,' said Pearson,

Soccer team. (*Blind Veterans UK*)

teaches the blinded man freedom and grace of movement and ease of carriage. Friday night is 'ball night' and Tuesday night is 'practice night', or 'learning night', and a great many ladies, among them professional teachers of dancing come on Tuesdays to teach the blinded soldiers to dance.[29]

Dances were held either outdoors, or in a marquee on the lawn, with competitions in which famous dancers were invited to act as judges and present the prizes. The Guards and other regiments sent their bands to play at such events.

Dancing became one of the most popular diversions with the blinded soldiers. [They] took up dancing with astonishing zest. How well they danced was remarkable. It was a genuine source of pleasure to them, a spontaneous outlet for that spirit of enjoyment which they found, after all, had not been lost. For partners the men had the willing help of the VADs— 'Sisters' as the soldiers always called them, and the lady coxswains.[30]

According to Ian Fraser, 'Soon, dance fever gripped St Dunstan's, and even some of the old soldiers were caught taking secret lessons.'[31]

Football was tried, with a bell placed inside the ball so that the blind men could locate its whereabouts, 'but the experiment never went further than causing some amusement.' Similarly, 'pushball', in which a team of men attempted to push a 10-foot high rubber ball the length of a field, and in between their opponents' (padded) goal posts, was not a great success.[32]

Although Pearson stressed that, in regard to training, the officers and men of St Dunstan's were to be treated equally, in respect of extramural life and activities, this was definitely

'Pushball'. (*Blind Veterans UK*)

St Dunstan's band. Alphonse van den Bosch, 7th Regt de Eigne, Belgian Infantry, is seated third from right. (*Blind Veterans UK*)

'Trial by Jury', December 1917. (*Blind Veterans UK*)

not the case. As already mentioned, the officers had their own separate living quarters, and separate sitting room within the Conservatory. They also had other separate facilities, as Pearson explains:

> They are provided with separate week-end winter quarters at Brighton, and they have at their disposal for summer week-ends a very beautiful house and grounds on one of the most picturesque reaches of the Thames. Here they go in for horseback riding and tandem bicycle racing, rowing, swimming, and all sorts of things in which you would never imagine a blind man could interest himself.[33]

So much for the body. What of the mind? How could the men's grey cells be stimulated? Pearson was a communicator par excellence. So, what was more natural than for him to make a point of addressing the men, on a regular basis, on current topics of interest? Noteworthy people were also invited to come and talk to them. In addition, a debating society was formed at which the Chief usually took the chair.

Music was a feature of St Dunstan's life, and the moving spirit behind this was Pearson's wife Ethel. Concerts were held in which professional instrumentalists and singers of the highest rank gave their services. However, the men were anxious to produce their own music,

On see-saw with VADs. (*Blind Veterans UK*)

and Pearson' wife Ethel, said Fraser, 'encouraged St Dunstaners to learn, to play, to perform… So we had, at various times, a brass band, a string band, a jazz band, and a full orchestra. We had performers on every known instrument, from the double bass to the penny whistle.'[34] Finally, 'a very able concert party of blind musicians' was formed, whose 'ceaseless round of engagements' raised considerable sums for the upkeep of St Dunstan's.[35] With clear pride, Pearson said, 'nearly every man at St Dunstans learns some kind of musical instrument, while a few of them with really good voices are going in seriously for singing.'[36]

Favourite indoor games were chess, draughts, dominoes and cards. The black draughts were smaller than the white so that the men might distinguish between them, and on reaching the other side of the board, instead of placing one draught on top of another as a sighted person would do, a 'double decker draught' was used. For dominoes, each gaming piece had raised instead of recessed bumps, and on Monday evenings there was a domino competition with prizes for the winners. Bridge was played with a sighted player to read out the name of each card as it was played[37]—each card being marked in the corner with an appropriate number of raised Braille dots.

Pearson painted a delightful picture of Sundays, which, after church service, were set aside for rest and relaxation. This was the day for taking a walk, if the weather permitted, and completing any unfinished tasks:

[It was] a great day for polishing off letters, and a man often remained firmly tapping at a typewriter till he had finished five or six long epistles, while others would make their way to the Outer Lounge and sit in comfortable armchairs round the big fire, or in the summer under the mulberry tree on the lawn.[38]

On the afternoon of 19 April 1915, St Dunstan's received a visit from Queen Alexandra, Princess Victoria, the Princess Royal, and Princess Maud. Queen Alexandra talked to the men, paid a visit to the workrooms, and was entertained at a concert at which all the performers were blind. She expressed her amazement at their cheerfulness and good spirits, and presented each of them with a large bunch of primroses tied with red, white, and blue ribbon.

The *St Dunstan's Review* (originally spelt 'Revue'), a record of the life of Dunstan's, was written, in the main, by the men themselves. Produced monthly and commencing in July 1915, it became a connecting link between St Dunstaners and those concerned with their welfare in all parts of the world.[39] The *Review* contained articles on such topics as rowing on the lake, Visitors' Day, horseback riding, poetry, and even trout fishing and golf. It also contained the inevitable parody on Rudyard Kipling's poem entitled 'If'. This particular version, written by one of the blinded officers, appeared in the edition of March 1917.

> If you should lose your sight while all about you
> Are keeping theirs, as soldiers often do;
> If you're alive when Huns have tried to rout you,
> And do not grumble when all's lost to view...

And it ended:

> If you can keep some hens, and never scare them,
> Of eggs you'll find you need not fear a dearth;
> If you can mend old boots, and people wear them,
> You'll feel you've made your mark upon this earth.
> If you get lost, make casts like any huntsman's;
> If you feel hopeless in the dark, don't mind,
> For when you've been a few months at St Dunstan's,
> You'll be a man, old chap, although you're blind.

On 11 June 1916, at the instigation of the Scottish National Institute for the Blind, a lease was obtained for Newington House, Edinburgh, in order to provide a facility in which those blinded servicemen from Scotland, who so wished, could be provided for.

Aftercare

When a man left St Dunstan's, it was by no means the end of his association with the hostel. He was provided with a complete set of tools, appropriate to the trade which he had been taught, and it was the responsibility of St Dunstan's Settlement Department to find him a suitable home, if required, and working premises. If he was married, he was given a weekly allowance for the period of one year, to assist him in the payment of his rent until he became established. Finally, Pearson himself made a point of keeping in touch by letter, both with the St Dunstaners and their relatives, whether in Britain or elsewhere in the world.

The Aftercare Department was headed by Ian Fraser. Fraser was wounded by an enemy bullet on 23 July 1916 during the Battle of the Somme; after his injury he walked to the field dressing-station with his company commander, unable to see, and believing his blindness to be only temporary. From here, he was taken to Le Touquet, to a casino which had been converted into a hospital. He was then sent back to England and admitted to the Officers' Ward at the 2nd London General Hospital, Chelsea. He would never see again.[1]

In October 1916, at Pearson's invitation, Fraser arrived at St Dunstan's to start his training and rehabilitation. Along with the other men, he learned typewriting and Braille, and for his specialist subject he chose carpentry. On 15 February 1917, Pearson wrote to Fraser's mother saying, 'I have had long talks with Ian lately, and have decided to train him up to assist me in working for the benefit of the blind.'[2] To this end, Fraser spent a month gaining experience in each of St Dunstan's different handicraft workshops.

As Pearson's assistant, Fraser was given the task, in autumn 1917, of designing a building to house a new Aftercare Department, of which he was to take charge. All those who had passed through St Dunstan's could thereby be monitored and assisted where necessary, for the remainder of their lives. According to Sidney Dark, there were local agents throughout the United Kingdom whose task it was to 'help the blind workman to obtain orders, and interest influential local people in his welfare'. He continues:

The raw materials are supplied at a reasonable price, and St Dunstan's purchases large quantities of leather, willows, yarn, wood, string, twine, and so on, to supply to the boot-repairers, the basket-makers, the mat-makers, the carpenters, and the net-makers. Likewise, specialists in the various crafts paid visits to the men on a regular basis, to examine their work and to make suggestions for improvements.[3]

The following correspondence, faithfully recorded by Dark (which he said was a mere fraction of what Pearson received in total), demonstrates just how appreciated, loved, and respected the Chief was, and how treasured his institution. Private W. H. J. Oxenham recalled the time when he was newly blinded and in hospital:

> I then thought that I was more or less no more good for this world, but I soon began to realize my error, and as time went on and I arrived at St Dunstan's this became more confirmed than ever, and I feel now full of confidence for the future.

Lieutenant Walter Millard declared that he was never happier than when he was 'at good old St Dunstan's':

> Nor are those days over, for you still keep so well in touch with us who have left that we feel that we are merely away on week-end holiday and have only to walk into the place to have it at our finger-ends.

Private F. C. Fleetwood stated that his wife had gone to market that day with 'mats and netted articles' which he had made. Said he, 'I hope she will sell out,' and then somewhat ruefully,

> I wonder how many of us fellows have a shot at getting their own dinner. To-day I am looking after a big fire, several pots and pans, doing a bit of baking, giving to the dog his dinner, and doing a bit of matting into the bargain.

Nevertheless, he confessed that he was secretly enjoying fulfilling the role of housewife!

The mother of a blinded Australian soldier wrote to tell Pearson that she was grateful to him beyond words,

> for the way my brave blind boy is able to get about so well and cheerfully, and my thanks to all those dear, kind people of St Dunstan's, who made life so pleasant for him when the darkest of shadows had threatened to overcast his life.[4]

Pearson spoke of letters which he had received from professional men who had returned to work; from businessmen who had recommended their 'important commercial undertakings'; from craftsmen who were earning livings comparable to sighted men in the same field of industry; from masseurs 'who are not only securing for themselves a comfortable competency, but are doing great good to others'; from poultry farmers who had created successful smallholdings; and from men who had found employment as secretaries or telephone exchange operators, who worked 'with a skill which is scarcely believable'.

> [They said] things about the work of St Dunstan's which come straight from the hearts of those who have benefited by it, and go straight to the hearts of those who have been privileged to be responsible for its initiation and management.

Pearson felt extraordinary pride in St Dunstaners going out to make a living for themselves, and he delighted in the encouraging letters he received.

Does any one in the world, I wonder, receive so many delightful letters as I do? The post brings me a never-ending stream of them from all parts of the United Kingdom and of the British Empire, telling of lives filled with undreamt of happiness, and of success truly marvellous, such as has never been won by blinded men before.[5]

Often there comes to my mental vision a picture of the writers as I first met them, hopeless, despairing, and unable to imagine that any good thing was left for them in life. And then I see in my mind's eye these happy, resolute, competent men, who, in spite of their handicap, are showing that they can do their fair share in the work of the world. It is a picture of joyous contemplation the like of which can, I think, has been given to few to conjure up.[6]

Such heartfelt gratitude from his men and the knowledge that they had 'made good' was to Pearson the greatest reward that he could have wished for.

The importance of aftercare cannot be overstated. One may imagine the St Dunstaner, being assailed by doubts and fears as he sets up on his own as telephonist, poultry farmer, boot repairer, or whatever. Will I succeed? And if not, how will I face the humiliation of failure? Suddenly, Pearson's voice and that of his instructor echo in his mind, encouraging, cajoling:

You are a St Dunstaner! Be strong! Be proud! Remember, St Dunstan's is always there in the background to support you if needs be. St Dunstan's will never let you down!

In March 1917, King George V visited (and took a particular interest in) St Dunstan's poultry farm. He was followed, in May, by the Prince of Wales and Princess Mary, and in the following year by Queen Mary, who was accompanied by her children Princess Mary and Prince Henry.

St Dunstan's, May 1917: The Prince of Wales, Sir Arthur Pearson, and Princess Mary. (*Blind Veterans UK*)

Gladys Cooper and St Dunstan's

English actress and celebrated beauty Gladys Constance Cooper was one of many celebrities who helped Pearson fundraise, not only for St Dunstan's but also for his Fresh Air Fund. Born at Lewisham, Kent, on 18 December 1888, Gladys's father, Charles F. W. Cooper, was a journalist and founding editor of *The Epicure*—a pioneering food and drink magazine. Her mother was Mabel (née Barnett). Gladys acknowledged that her 'parents belonged to the literary and artistic set of their day'. As for herself, she declared, 'I do not think I had any stage heredity in me, yet I suppose I must have always possessed, unconsciously, a sense of drama.'[1]

It was a friend of Gladys's, Mary Henessey (herself an aspiring actress) who encouraged Gladys to go for a 'voice trial' at London's Vaudeville Theatre in the Strand. The outcome was that, in 1905, she made her stage debut, touring with British actor, playwright, theatre manager, and producer Seymour Hicks, in his musical *Bluebell in Fairyland*. From this, she progressed to pantomime, before joining theatre manager George Edwardes at London's Gaiety Theatre in 1907. Gladys subsequently appeared in plays by George Bernard Shaw, John Galsworthy, and others, performing at various theatres including The Royalty, Drury Lane, and Wyndhams.

During the war, Gladys's husband, Herbert Buckmaster, served for three and a half years on the Western Front as an officer in the 12th Reserve Regiment of Cavalry. Meanwhile, she continued with her acting career. In late 1914, Gladys travelled with Seymour Hicks and his company to France, where they staged concerts for British, French, and Belgian troops.

At about that time Gladys attended what she described as 'the finest ball I have ever been to', hosted by Pearson at London's Savoy Hotel in order to raise funds for St Dunstan's. She said,

> I was able to be of very considerable help to him, and sold heaps of tickets and got a very large number of people interested. As everyone knows, St Dunstan's was the entire work and creation of Sir Arthur Pearson. Blind himself, he had the keenest sympathy and the tenderest understanding of the sufferings and deprivations of the blind.[2]
>
> There is no doubt that he is a wonderful man. He was completely blind, but he had a marvellous way of looking after himself. He knew, for example, exactly where his tea-cup could be safely put at the edge of a table, and he never seemed to fumble with things. We frequently talked about being blind, and I remember once saying to him, 'I can't begin to understand what it means—I can't enter into things with blind people as you can,' and him

Gladys Cooper. (*Sally Hardy*)

replying, 'Ah, but then, you see, I am with the blind.' That was what he always said to other blind men: 'I am with you.'[3]

In fact, Gladys had met Pearson in the pre-war years, and it was through him that she had become associated with the Fresh Air Fund. 'I hope as long as I live to be associated with these two great philanthropic schemes,' she declared.[4]

Neville Pearson was invited by his father to attend a dance at St Dunstan's. This included a prize giving at which Gladys was to present the prizes. Having set eyes on her, and despite the fact that she was his senior by almost a decade, Neville declared, 'That is the girl I intend one day to marry'.[5]

Pearson and the Secret of His Success

It has to be remembered that admission to St Dunstan's had, of necessity, to be a selective process, and that there were many men who, apart from being blind, were simply too badly injured in mind or body, or both, to be able to participate in its training programme. But of those who were admitted, 'between 90 and 95 per cent ... could—and did—earn a living, or at any rate, add substantially to their pensions after they had left'.[1] There were several aspects that contributed to this achievement.

The fellowship of the blind
Right from the start, Pearson had realized the importance of bringing all the blinded servicemen together under one roof. This was in order not only that they might avail themselves of the specialized services which St Dunstan's had to offer, but equally importantly, that they should bond together, in a new 'Regiment of the Blind', where they could give one another help, encouragement, and emotional support, as the new challenge of 'learning to be blind' confronted them.

One may imagine a newly blinded man being sent straight home from hospital and finding himself in the company of loved ones and friends. He quickly realizes the futility of attempting to describe what he has endured. He therefore chooses to suppress his feelings, and having done so, feels both frustrated and isolated.

Compare this with St Dunstan's, where, in the company of comrades, he could relax, share a cigarette or a joke, and even discuss the war in the knowledge that he was being listened to by men who knew what he was talking about. In this way, friendships were built up, both at work and at play. The men shared their experiences of sightlessness, and worked together to overcome their common problems.

A New Zealand soldier once wrote, anonymously, of life in the trenches: 'I will never forget, the stimulus which has kept me going ... human fellowship'.[19] The same was surely true of Pearson's St Dunstaners. And this sense of comradeship was reinforced when a serving serviceman came to visit—as many did—and boosted their morale.

Treatment of shell shock
During the First World War, as many as 5 per cent of soldiers were evacuated from the battlefield because they were suffering from shell shock—otherwise known as 'war neurosis'—and it is highly likely that a number of St Dunstaners had suffered, and continued to suffer, likewise. This condition (which today would be called 'post-traumatic stress disorder') was characterized

by depression, excessive irritability, guilt (at having survived, when so many others had not), recurrent nightmares, flashbacks to traumatic scenes, and over-reaction to sudden noises.

In the first year of the war, many of the victims of shell shock were regarded as insane. As the war progressed, there was a more enlightened approach and it was recognized that what such patients required was rest, quietude, and relaxation. It was not until 1917 that intensive six-week courses were created to teach medical officers how to recognize and treat shell shock casualties in the forward battle areas. Those admitted to St Dunstan's with shell shock would undoubtedly have received the same care and attention.

Psychological support

It is significant that Pearson makes no mention of the word 'psychologist' in his book *Victory over Blindness*, his record of life and work at St Dunstan's. Even its penultimate chapter—entitled 'The Psychology of the Blinded Soldier'—was written, not by a psychologist, but by author and journalist Richard King Huskinson, who was also one of St Dunstan's volunteer helpers. This is not to say that a trained psychologist would not have had an important contribution to make. However, Pearson evidently believed that he could manage without one.

A convivial atmosphere

In the armed services, the men had been subjected to strict discipline with an overwhelming array of rules and regulations. St Dunstan's also had its rules, and if a man broke them, he was disciplined. If the breach was sufficiently serious, he was asked to leave the organization. However, in the main, the atmosphere was overwhelmingly one of warmth and conviviality.

One of the pleasures that the men enjoyed, both in the services and at St Dunstan's, was a cigarette or a pipe of tobacco. Said Pearson,

> Visitors to the hostel were generally surprised to find that the habit of smoking was almost universal among the men. Certainly one of the pleasures of smoking is lost to one who cannot see the smoke, yet it remains not only a pleasure but a solace to the blinded man. At St Dunstan's the men smoked at work as well as at other times. Pipes were not commonly used; it was the cigarette that was popular.[2]

Incentivisation

Men in training wore a badge 'in the shape of a blue oblong, surrounded by laurel sprays upon which were the words, "Soldiers and Sailors blinded in the War. St. Dunstan's stands for Victory over Blindness."' But Pearson, ever anxious to incentivize his St Dunstaners, decided that a further badge was needed for those who had passed from training to aftercare, and he invited suggestions. The outcome was a 'graduates' badge, with flaming torch encircled by a shield, and the name 'St. Dunstan's' emblazoned across it.[3]

Spiritual support

The spiritual needs of the men were catered for by an Anglican or a Roman Catholic clergyman who conducted the church services on Sundays. In addition, chaplains were always on hand to talk to the men.

Blind teachers

Both Pearson and the men knew how important it was, psychologically, for the men to be taught by blind teachers:

> When a blinded man with that horrible feeling of helplessness which first overcomes him, particularly if he tries to do something, finds that the man who is teaching him is blind himself, he thinks at once: 'I am not being asked to do something which is impossible, by someone who does not understand. I am being shown the right way—this man who is blind knows what he is doing and I too can do it'.[4]

Furthermore, if a St Dunstaner was found to have a particular aptitude for teaching, and to possess sufficient skill in his craft, then he was swiftly recruited into the ranks of the teaching staff. Such a person was Tommy Rogers, who taught typewriting and whose career at St Dunstan's would last for twenty-six years.

Friends, family, and the danger of mollycoddling

Pearson encouraged family members to visit the men, and facilitated their doing so by paying their train or omnibus fares and inviting them to stay for a few days, or even for a week, at the organization's expense. And when visitors arrived the Chief was not slow to explain his ideas to them.

> I had sometimes to insist that a newly blinded man's worst enemy was apt to be his own loving wife, or mother, or sister. For the tender desire to wait on a blinded man, to do everything for him, to remove all difficulties from his path, has the effect of preventing him from making the wonderful discovery of all he can do for himself.[5]
>
> To the public I say: do not pity these blinded men, give them all the sympathy in the world, give them all the help you possibly can, encourage them in their growing spirit of independence; when you walk with them guide them as little as possible, when you talk to them do not talk to them as men cut off from all the beauty of the world and of the passing interests of the day. If they have set themselves to forget what they have suffered and what they are suffering, is it for you to remind them?

In other words, family and friends, however well intentioned, could easily undo all the good work done by St Dunstan's, thereby hindering a man's recovery rather than facilitating it. On the positive side, relatives were invited to participate in parts of the relevant training courses themselves. This was because certain occupations required that a blind man receive some assistance from a sighted person.

Finally, despite Pearson's strictures on the dangers of mollycoddling, the love, care, and devotion of family and friends was enormously important. In this new environment, acts of kindness, however small, assumed great significance. The example is given of a soldier who is sitting in the garden one day, talking to a newly arrived comrade. The comrade is complaining that his lips are painful and oversensitive—having previously been singed by the blast from a shell—to the extent that he can no longer enjoy a cigarette. 'Now don't you fret, mate,' says the soldier, reaching into his pocket. 'I've got just the thing for you. I designed it myself. A tiny acorn cup holds the ciggy, like so, and then this little hollow stalk fits into the hole that I bored into the cup, like so. And there you have it—a ciggy holder!' A match is struck. The comrade feels the tiny tube between his lips. It is so tiny that he can tolerate it. He takes a deep breath. Then he coughs and splutters. 'How does that feel, mate?' asks the soldier anxiously. 'Good!' replies the comrade, spluttering and gasping for breath. 'Real good!'[20]

Womenfolk: a tonic for the men
Women were another vital factor, and Pearson himself was fulsome in his praise of, and appreciation for, the multitude of females—including the dedicated nursing staff—who played such a pivotal role in the rehabilitation process. In fact, even before he had arrived at St Dunstan's,

> the soldier who had lost his sight was given most tender care by the Sisters, Superintendents and Nurses [in the hospitals in which they found themselves].[6]
>
> One thinks of the women workers especially—of how they contributed to the happiness of the men, of how they gladdened their hearts, taking the trouble to understand them, and to bring just the right kind of cheer and sympathy to bear on their problems.

Pearson also acknowledged that most of the work of St Dunstan's was 'gladly undertaken' by women. The VADs, for example,

> supervised the men's arrivals, departures, and holidays. They organized cars and trains to take them to the theatre; on excursions—for they received many invitations in the outside world—and on week-end outings. They occupied themselves in reading letters, or opening parcels which the men received in the post. Writing letters for them when the need arose; reading aloud to them, and, in short, helping in every way to entertain them in their hours of leisure.

Women also attended to the laundry, darned socks, undertook sewing repairs, made the beds, did the housework, and waited on the men at table. As St Dunstan's expanded, there were eventually some 600 women who 'devoted all or a great part of their time to this labour of love'—the majority being volunteers.

As for Matron, just as the men viewed Pearson as a father figure, so equally they regarded her as a mother. (In fact, to many who were 'mere lads,' said Pearson, she was 'the Supreme Mother.') The same applied to the nursing sisters and trained nurses who presided over the dispensaries. They did so 'with a mother's care and more than a mother's skill.'[7]

The female secretary who dealt with administration also earned the men's devotion. In fact, in all the offices of St Dunstan's there were 'women doing work on which ... the happiness of the men depended'.

Youth of the St Dunstaners

Consultant ophthalmologist Arnold Lawson, pointed out that the re-education of a man becomes increasingly difficult as he grows older and more set in his ways, whereas the men of St Dunstan's, in the main, had youth on their side:

> It was this spirit of youth that was the chief asset in the production of that wonderful cheeriness which so pervaded St Dunstan's during the war, and so astonished all who went there. The society of comrades severely maimed helped in a very great measure; but neither the society of comrades nor the sympathy and help of all who worked at St Dunstan's would have brought that laughter and that brightness if St Dunstan's had been peopled by old men instead of men mostly in the prime of youth.[21]

Pearson summed up the situation when he referred to the 'cheerful … active, healthy, eager, young blind men who were learning in an atmosphere of good fellowship to start life again. It is a claim which I am justified in making, that St Dunstan's is one of the most cheerful places in the kingdom.'[22]

Pearson's aura of positivity

The original motto of St Dunstan's was somewhat uninspiring: 'What the eye does not see the heart does not grieve about'. However, a new motto that was more inspiring was adopted: 'Victory Over Blindness'. This was also the title which Pearson had given to one of his books, and it epitomized his indomitable spirit. (Another of Pearson's books was entitled *Conquest Over Blindness*). Sidney Dark happened to overhear a conversation in which Matron mentioned to Pearson that one of the men was despondent. 'Despondent, what on earth has he got to be despondent about?' came the reply. The word 'despondency' was, apparently, not a part of the Chief's vocabulary!

In his utterances and exhortations, Pearson may be accused of being over-optimistic, of painting too rosy a picture, perhaps of being in denial. But in fairness, it was his role to encourage and inspire. Moreover, the testimony of his men, what they achieved, and the affection and esteem in which they held him, all indicate that the message he gave out was absolutely the correct one.

Inspired by Pearson's example, the men almost invariably found that they developed a new surge of interest and energy, which was accompanied by an improvement in their general health. Occasionally however, there were bad days—days of immense frustration, even despair. Until the friendly voice of the Chief, or their instructor, or a VAD, or Matron, uttered words of gentle encouragement, so helping to soothe the spirit and dispel that self-destroying anger which welled up within them from time to time.

The distinction between 'Affliction' and 'Handicap'

Pearson was shocked one day when a deputation of teachers and pupils arrived from an institution for the blind in the north of England, and its chairman referred to his blind pupils as 'the little afflicted ones'. Pearson gave a withering rebuke:

Sir C. Arthur Pearson, Bt.,
English School, *c.* 1920. (*The
Hon. Mrs Egerton-Warburton*)

If you tell a man often enough that he is afflicted he will become afflicted and will adopt the mental and physical attitude befitting that soul-destroying word.[9]

Instead, he suggested the alternative word 'handicap', for this was something which could be overcome, even if a handicapped person cannot perform tasks as quickly as normal.[10] (Today, the word 'disability' might be seen to be more appropriate.)

Pearson the self-reliant

Pearson lived his life with characteristic gusto and panache, and refused to seek help for himself if he could possibly avoid it. 'I set myself to live as active and as independent a life as possible,' he said. He was equally determined that his men should do the same so that they might 'escape from that passive half-life which seemed so commonly accepted as inevitable'.[11]

Ian Fraser, however, described how the unknowing Pearson was receiving a certain amount of help behind the scenes, for example, when it came to taking his meals:

He refused all help, and claimed he could deal with anything that was put on his plate, from a lamb chop to a chicken wing. [However] He only got away with it because jolly good care was taken to see that no bone was ever put on his plate. In fairness, I must say that this was not done with his connivance.[12]

This had an unforeseen consequence when, said Fraser, one of the men who was attempting to follow Pearson's example became 'over-inspired', with the result that he 'got into an awful mess trying to cut up his tie!'

Pearson was also aware of the importance of preserving the dignity of the men, and when a blind officer asked him if 'some device could be invented to enable blind men to play billiards', he regarded this as a step too far:

For Heaven's sake, don't let us make ourselves ridiculous. It's absurd to try and play a game like billiards, which absolutely depends on keen sight. There are so many things that we can do, without making asses of ourselves.[8]

Pearson's attention to detail

Pearson was meticulous by nature, both in appearance and in his work, and he expected his men to be likewise.

People seem apt to think that if a man is blind he must necessarily be untidy. He very often is. But as St Dunstaners know, I attach the greatest importance to tidiness and smartness.[13]

There were limits, however, to what even Pearson could achieve unaided, and he freely acknowledged the help given to him by Irene Mace, his personal assistant and guide (and who subsequently became Commandant of the VADs.)[14]

Pearson: one who did not suffer fools gladly

Although Fraser described Pearson as being 'generous and warm-hearted', there was also another side to his nature.

He was quick-tempered as well as quick-witted, and if you did not see his point as quickly as he thought you should, he was liable to flare up and blow you out of the room. But the mood quickly passed, and he was never too big to apologize.[15]

Pearson, champion of his men

For disabled service personnel, the awarding of pensions was in accordance with an antiquated system dating back to the year 1754, in which the Chelsea Commissioners, in conjunction with the Army Council, acted as adjudicators.

Up until February 1915, the maximum compensation paid to a serviceman who had been totally blinded as a result of war service was half a crown (2s 6d) per day, or 17s 6d per week.[16] By March 1915, the amount had been increased to 25s per week for a private soldier, rising to up to 40s per week for a warrant officer class one. In December 1916, the various pension departments were brought under the single umbrella of the Ministry of Pensions. Nonetheless, said Fraser, this system proved 'hopelessly impracticable, creating suspicion among disabled soldiers and causing lengthy delays'.[17]

The battle was now joined by Pearson who fought, successfully, for his blind men to receive, in addition to their basic pension, an additional 'attendant allowance'. However, the government now created further problems by insisting that a blinded man must prove that his disability was directly attributable to war service. This presented a difficulty for those who had pre-existing eye conditions when they joined the military.

A compromise was reached when pension eligibility was extended to men discharged from the Army on account of their having a pre-existing disease which had been aggravated by war service. However, because of the narrow interpretation by the Ministry of the word 'aggravation', many legitimate claims were refused. Finally, as a result of pressure put upon it, the Ministry set up an appeals board, and later a pensions appeal tribunal. St Dunstan's responded by establishing its own dedicated pensions office, and appointed its own pensions officer to represent its men.[18] This proved a great success.

In his continuing battles with the Ministry, Pearson had a staunch ally in Arnold Lawson, who spoke on behalf of the men at the pensions appeal tribunals, pointing out that those with defective eyesight ought never to have been admitted into the armed services in the first place. It was, therefore, 'adding insult to injury for the Tribunal to disclaim responsibility for such persons'.

The fact that Pearson (and others) was prepared to go to such lengths for his men, was yet another sign that in the Chief they had a resolute leader and a steadfast and true friend in whom they could have every confidence. But there were other factors which made St Dunstan's the success that it undoubtedly was.

The 'Chief' Visits the Front

Pearson was aware that his blindness was actually an advantage to him in his dealings with the men; it gave him a unique insight into the kind of difficulties they faced. But in another respect, he was at a disadvantage in that unlike them, he had no first-hand experience of war. He therefore applied for permission to visit the Western Front, and in August 1917, the fifty-one-year-old's wish was granted.

Vimy Ridge, 7½ miles north-east of Arras, had been in German hands until 9 April, when it was successfully stormed by Canadian and British forces. There was a special reason why Pearson had chosen this particular theatre of war—it was the very place that his son Neville, had very recently been wounded. Neville had left Eton College on 20 December 1916 and departed straightaway for the Western Front, where he served for a period of thirteen months with the Royal Field Artillery (Territorial Force).[1]

Pearson arrived in company with his guide and his son Neville. The rain was incessant and the ground muddy and slippery, just as it had been during the attack. Based on what his companions had told him, Pearson described the Ridge as being '360 feet high' and holding 'a very commanding position'. 'The ground,' continued Pearson, speaking as if he were a normally sighted person,

> is almost indescribable. It is simply a succession of gigantic holes [created by shells and mines] and jagged crevices. Three batteries behind us were firing away over the Ridge, and we could see the shells crashing on the land just beyond the embankment of the Railway that runs between Lens and Arras.

The three men ascended the Ridge. However, after only two to three minutes, they came under enemy fire and were obliged to take cover in a dugout. Having remained in the dugout for about 10 minutes they emerged, but no sooner had they done so, when another shell landed on the very spot where they had previously been standing.

> This one was a good deal too close to be comfortable. I felt a distinct shock, and was splashed all over with mud, and I had the further honour and glory of receiving a wound on the head from a stone. Wound is, perhaps, rather a large word, for it only took the form of a pretty sharp rap, which raised a bit of a bump, but it enabled me to realize just a little bit what the real thing must feel like.[2]

While in France, Pearson visited a tank depot—or 'Tankeydrome'—and a camp for German prisoners of war. He also visited Lieutenant General Sir Henry Sinclair Horne, Commander of the British First Army and the 'School of Scouting, Observation, and Sniping' at Linghem in the Pas-de-Calais, in which he took a keen interest. This was the first such school to be established by the British Army, and it had been created by his 'old friend' Hesketh Prichard, who, as already mentioned, had been dispatched by Pearson in late 1900 to hunt for the giant sloth of Patagonia.

Following his experience at Vimy Ridge, Pearson declared, 'I am convinced that I have just as clear an idea of what is going on at the Front as has anyone else who has been there lately.' This, of course, was a colossal overstatement. Nevertheless, he believed that having visited the Front and experienced something of what his St Dunstaners had been through, he could better empathize with his men, and forge 'another link between him[self] and his blinded soldiers'.[3] As for his St Dunstaners, they probably greeted his visit to the Front with horror and incredulity. What if the Chief had been killed? What then?

Further Developments at St Dunstan's

Once again, the minutes of the meetings of St Dunstan's Committee give a valuable insight into life at St Dunstan's as the war progressed.

In September 1917, Mr Charles E. Rose resigned from the Committee and from his post as Honorary Superintendent of Works & Sports. He was succeeded by Mr Sansome. Mr A. D. Hall, 'whose long experience in the industries taught in the workshops would be of the upmost value,' was appointed Works Manager. Meanwhile, Mr and Mrs Anderton were appointed to superintend Townsend House: her duties were to teach Braille in the classrooms and his, to manage the poultry farm. The Committee resolved that 'poultry men' should also be taught 'rabbit-keeping' (as already mentioned—but whether the rabbits were to be kept as pets, or for their meat and/or pelts is not disclosed!).

The Bungalow Annexe now had 140 residents, and West House, Brighton, was 'in full swing'.[1] By 30 October 1917, numbers at the Bungalow Annexe had increased to 184.[8] By November 1917, virtually all the space in the grounds of St Dunstan's had been taken up by new buildings, and plans were in hand for the extension of the Torquay Annexe, and for a temporary building to be erected adjoining the Bungalow Annexe to provide sleeping quarters for sixty men. (Part of the latter building would extend into Regent's Park.) Three houses in Cornwall Terrace had been acquired 'with a view to extension of accommodation for men learning massage'. Regarding the new additions in St Dunstan's grounds, Pearson said,

> Otto Kahn gave me absolute *carte blanche* to erect any buildings and effect any alterations that I thought fit to make. At the moment of writing the once beautiful gardens of St Dunstan's are almost covered with workshops, classrooms, offices, storehouses, chapels [two—one Anglican, the other Roman Catholic] and recreation rooms, while additions to the house extend on all sides, and the vast building which we call the Bungalow Annexe covers one of the fields.[2]

Pearson might also have added that the classrooms and workshops were connected by covered walkways, and that the extensions also included men's dormitories; a dispensary; a tobacco store; pensions department offices; offices of the Settlement Department (charged with placing men in suitable positions of employment); an Aftercare Department; and the secretaries' offices where 'with the help of a large staff, an immense correspondence' was conducted.[3]

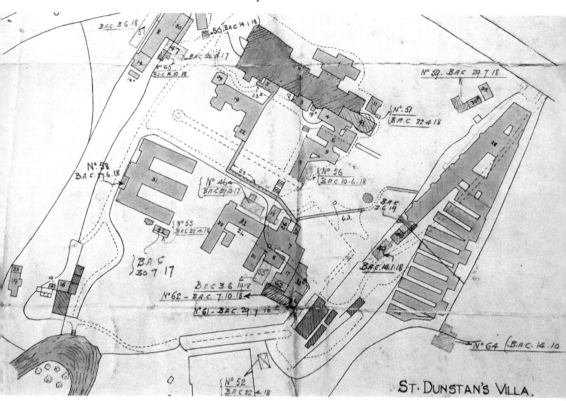

Plan of alterations and additions to St Dunstan's, 20 July 1917. (*London Metropolitan Archive*)

1	Dormitories in front of house	23a	Office next to dispensary
2	Workshops in side field	24	Two rooms off Braille room
3	Extension of dining room	25	Office for Aftercare dept.
4	Ditto to dining room, bath, lavatories	26	Office off Braille room
5	Dispensary off lounge	27	Cloakroom off Braille room
6	Dormitory on terrace next to conservatory	28	Annexe in field on N. side
7	Braille room in grounds	29	Massage classrooms
8	Addition to ditto for typists	30	Nil
9	Office for Aftercare next to No. 6	31	New workshop in grounds
10	Lecture room at farm	32	New Braille and net rooms
11	Dressing room next to conservatory	33	Lecture room at farm
12	Matron's office on terrace	34	Cloakroom cancelled
13	Dormitories and offices next to No. 6	35	Storeroom for annexe
14	Addition to workshop S.E. end	36	Linen room to annexe
14a	Store shed next to workshop S.E. end	37	Nil
15	Roman Catholic chapel	38	Nil
16	Roof to yard at farm	39	Cloakroom adjoining lounge
17	Addition to net room	40	Quiet lounge (annexe)
18	Two lecture rooms & office at farm	41	New office on conservatory sight
19	Quiet lounge on top terrace	42	Woodstores adjoining 31
20	Addition to workshop N.W. end	43	Covered way Braille room to annexe
21	Addition to Braille room	51	Lavatory
22	Chapel next to quiet lounge	52	Office & store for sports materials
23	Covered way to Braille room	53	Timber store additions to No. 42

Matron Miss Frances Hughes (second from left) with men and staff, 1917. (*Blind Veterans UK*)

Just before he had lost his sight completely, Pearson had said to his wife, 'I shall soon be blind, but I will never be *a* blind man, I am going to be *the* blind man.'[4] Now he could claim, with justification, that he had achieved his aim: for he declared St Dunstan's to be the largest concern which he had ever presided over, larger even than his newspaper and publishing empire. On 20 September his wonderful achievement was officially recognized, and Pearson received the congratulations of the Committee 'on the Honour recently conferred upon him by the King of the Grand Cross of the British Empire'.

On 4 December 1917, Pearson informed the Committee of General Sir Francis Lloyd's visit to St Dunstan's, and of his 'distribution of distinctions [presumably medals] gained by nine men'. A letter had also been received from Canadian St Dunstaners Edwin Baker and Alexander Viets, Mr Sherman Swift of the Canadian Free Library for the Blind, and Dr Charles R. Dickson, Secretary General of the Canadian National Institute of the Blind (CNIB), 'giving full particulars of the proposed arrangements being formulated in Canada for the training of blinded Canadian soldiers'. In the letter, Baker and Viets both expressed 'gratitude and appreciation' for the training which they had received at St Dunstan's.[5] Baker was later to be appointed Secretary of the Blinded Soldiers Department of the Invalided Soldiers Commission, Canada, and Dr Dickson later offered to act as sole representative for St Dunstan's in Canada.

Maintaining strong links across the Commonwealth was very important to Pearson, and he was careful to ensure that Commonwealth soldiers received the same opportunity to go to St Dunstan's as their British colleagues. In 1918 nine Canadians who had been returned to Canada without having been given the opportunity of training at St Dunstan's arrived at the hostel. St Dunstan's staff also reflected these close international links when Corporal Charles Purkis (34th Battalion), a blinded Canadian soldier who had trained at St Dunstan's, was appointed Poultry Instructor to the CNIB. Pearson also made sure that there was adequate aftercare for all blinded Australians trained at St Dunstan's on their return to Australia.

On 29 January 1918, Miss Hughes resigned as Matron of St Dunstan's; sadly, she had suffered a severe nervous breakdown, perhaps due to pressure of work.[6] She was succeeded by Miss Holland. Also, Mrs Craven resigned as Matron of the Bungalow Annexe; she was succeeded by Miss Edith Wood.[7] There was further bad news in February, when due to recent mysterious (unspecified) 'happenings' at the Torquay Annexe, all of its residents were transferred to London. Meanwhile the NIB acquired 38 Lee Terrace, Blackheath, adjoining the Blackheath Annexe they already owned. It was reported that 'arrangements [were] being made to join the houses and grounds to make one complete establishment of the two.'[8]

Up until March 1918 the stance of Pearson's periodical *Pearson's Magazine*, had been opposed to the war. Now, there was a U-turn and the decision was made 'to join in support of the war aims' of US President Woodrow Wilson and the British Labour Party.[9] Pearson, however, was grateful for help from whichever political party, and in June 1918 Conservative politician Lord Chaplin joined the Committee. Delegates from the Inter-Allied Conference (Conference of the Socialist Parties of the Allied Powers) visited St Dunstan's in April, along with Otto Kahn and various members of the royal family. The following month Kahn wrote to Pearson:

What has aroused my admiration … above all [is] the spirit of cheer, buoyancy, and courage which pervades the atmosphere of the place, and which is plainly apparent in the attitude and facial expression of the men and in the very manner of their firm and determined step.

The fact that this admirable demonstration of British organizing genius and practical humanity is being carried on in a house belonging to an American citizen [which Kahn had become in 1917], I like to regard as symbolic of that close and lasting and effective union between the two countries.[10]

In early June 1918 St Dunstan's was smitten with sadness: on the 13th the Committee recorded its 'sincere grief' at the sudden death of Miss E. W. Austin and its appreciation of 'her organization of the Braille teaching department of St Dunstan's'. However, there was happy news also, and on 16 July the Committee congratulated Miss Irene Mace and Captain Ian Fraser on their forthcoming marriage.

Demand for accommodation continued to grow throughout the summer of 1918; extensions to West House, Brighton would provide an additional thirty beds and Pearson reported that the St Leonard's Annexe at Cheltenham in Gloucestershire, together with the Ilkley Annexe in Yorkshire, had now opened for business. No. 14 Sussex Place, a house lent by Mr Meyer, was also shortly to be opened as an isolation hospital annexe to St Dunstan's.[11] As for graduate St Dunstaners, four shorthand-typists and telephonists had found employment with 'well-known London firms',[12] and fourteen men and one officer had sat and passed the recent examination in massage and all had since obtained employment at military hospitals.[13]

On 23 July 1918, which was the second anniversary of his having been blinded, Ian Fraser and Irene Mace were married. (Irene had first met the newly blinded Fraser when she had visited him at the 2nd London General Hospital, Chelsea, on Pearson's behalf, to invite Fraser to join St Dunstan's.)

In that year, the Federation of Grocers' Associations purchased St Dunstan's' Annexe, West House, Brighton, and presented it to the organization. Here, it should be noted that Pearson's sister Marion had worked at Queen's Road Annexe, Brighton, prior to becoming the first Matron of West House from 1917, until she retired through ill health in 1923. Pearson's other sister, Olive, was Matron ('Commandant') of Queen's Road Annexe prior to becoming Matron of St Leonard's Annexe, Cheltenham, from 1917 until its closure in 1923. After its closure she declared, 'I shall never forget the six years I spent with my St Dunstan's boys, to whom I still feel I belong — indeed, as my brother's sister I could never feel otherwise.'[14]

Also in that year, Ruby Smith, daughter of the Head Gardener, and now aged six, showed her concern for the men by making a collection for them. This prompted the following response from Pearson:

Dear little Ruby,
The collecting box you brought me yesterday had 18s/3d in it. I think it is very sweet of you to collect this for the blinded soldiers.
Yours sincerely, Arthur Pearson[15]

The Armistice and Beyond

Does it matter? —losing your sight?...
There's such splendid work for the blind;
And people will always be kind,
As you sit on the terrace remembering
And turning your face to the light.

Do they matter? —those dreams from the pit?...
You can drink and forget and be glad,

And people won't say that you're mad;

For they'll know that you've fought for your country
And no one will worry a bit.

'Does it Matter?' by Siegfried Sassoon, 1917

The war ended on 11 November 1918 with the signing of the Armistice. By this time, said Pearson, in excess of 600 St Dunstaners had 'learned to be blind and had returned to their homes. Nearly seven hundred were still in training at St Dunstan's and at the various annexes, and nearly two hundred were still in hospital [awaiting admission].' They included seventy Australians, sixty-three Canadians, twenty New Zealanders, and ten South Africans. Said Fraser,

St Dunstan's has looked after practically all the men of the Home and Dominion Forces who were blinded in the Great War and about half the Scotsmen. The other Scotsmen went to Newington House, Edinburgh, in the main because they lived in or near Edinburgh and wished to be near their folk at the time when they were blinded.[1]

Pearson pointed out just how large the organization which he had founded had now become.[2] No less than 595 women were employed including 'matrons; VADs; nurses; teachers of Braille, typewriting and music; regular visitors, and those who came to read to the men and take them for walks, and secretaries'. The male staff of 293 included 'the adjutants; the oculists; the doctors; the chaplains; the workshops' teachers; poultry-farm instructors; accountants;

orderlies; walkers; masseurs; chauffeurs; porters; gardeners; scouts; and those engaged in the Pensions, the Settlement, and the Aftercare Departments.'[3]

For five and a half years Pearson had strained every sinew to make St Dunstan's a success, not only in the United Kingdom, but globally. And this was not his only concern, for he was also President of the NIB and had connections with homes for the blind in Chester, Bristol, Liverpool, Manchester, Bradford, Leeds, and Cardiff. In Hertfordshire he had encouraged the creation of the Chorleywood College for Girls with little or no sight. His enthusiasm captured the imagination of the nation, and his success at fundraising enabled the NIB to open the 'Sunshine Home' for blind babies, also at Chorleywood.

In January 1919 the seemingly indefatigable Pearson travelled to Canada and the USA. The Evergreen Red Cross Institute for the Blind had been founded in 1917, and during the First World War its headquarters were 'Evergreen', North Charles Street, Baltimore, Maryland—a property which had been loaned to the US Government by Mrs T. Harrison Garrett. Here, US soldiers and sailors who had been blinded in the war underwent training and rehabilitation. (In late June 1917 the first US combat troops had arrived in France, and by Summer 1918 their numbers had risen to about one million.)

On the 16 January, the Institute gave a dinner in Pearson's honour. For his part, he told his US audience how, on his recent visit to Toronto, Ontario, Canada, twenty-eight people had sat down to dinner, including 'twenty-seven blind hosts—soldiers who had returned to Canada from St Dunstan's, and one blind guest—myself'. The Canadian National Institute for the Blind (CNIB), he predicted, would 'alter the whole situation for the many thousand blind people of the Dominion'.

As for his British St Dunstaners, there were currently a total of 704 men in residence, with an additional 150 men in hospital 'waiting to come to us just as soon as they recover from their injuries'.[4] As for those who had graduated from St Dunstan's, sixty-four had qualified as masseurs and found permanent employment either in hospitals or in private practice, and a further forty-two had qualified as shorthand typists and were currently employed 'in large business houses throughout the United Kingdom. They are doing ordinary work and earning ordinary wages—most of them more than they did when they could see.' Finally, Pearson was

Queen Alexandra, with Pearson to her left, December 1918. (*Blind Veterans UK*)

Staff, Bungalow Annexe, November 1918. (*Blind Veterans UK*)

delighted to inform his US audience that, 'three hundred and fifty of the men of St Dunstan's have been married since they became blind and a topping lot of girls they have got, too'.[5]

On 25 March 1919, having returned to the UK, Pearson enlightened the Committee about his visit to North America, where he had discussed with US authorities the various occupations which were open to the blinded men; and with the Canadian authorities the arrangements made with regard to the aftercare of Canadian St Dunstaners. On a sadder note, he informed the Committee of Otto Kahn's decision that St Dunstan's must be closed down 'by the end of this year', but that Kahn would permit the Bungalow Annexe, workshops, classrooms, etc. 'to remain in use until the end of 1920, or longer, if required'.[6]

On 15 May 1919 a relieved Pearson told the Committee that St Dunstan's tenure of the College Annexe would continue until March 1920. Had this not been the case, the outcome for the organization would have been catastrophic. In that month of May, Mr William G. Askew was appointed Pensions Officer.[7] Askew would serve St Dunstan's for an astonishing thirty-six years, and be responsible for winning 85 per cent of cases which had gone to the Appeals Tribunal. On the topic of pensions, Pearson noted that a large number of applicants to St Dunstan's were men whose blindness was due to venereal disease. He therefore recommended to the Committee that such men should not be admitted 'unless the Ministry of Pensions acknowledge the disability to be aggravated by military service'.[8]

In July 1919 an article appeared in the *Daily Mirror* newspaper under the heading 'St Dunstan's heroine: Story of a Plucky Nurse and a Capsized Boat'. It indicated that leisure activities arranged for St Dunstaners did not always go according to plan. The drama, which involved four blind St Dunstaners who were rowing (presumably on Regent's Park Lake), and their VAD coxswain, was described by George Gibson:

> After the boat had capsized Miss Zoe Stein [a St Dunstan's VAD nurse] supported one of the men in the water, and by her cries directed the others to the boat, when they managed to catch hold of the riggers. Nurse Stein was very reluctant to speak of her plucky act. 'The boat went over by a heavy wash, and we were all thrown into the water,' she said. 'Porter, who could not swim, was nearest to me, and we went down together. As we came up he laid his hand on my shoulder. By shouting I was able to guide the men to the boat, and we were taken out of the water about ten minutes later.'

In fact, it was Gibson himself (the holder of the King's Medal for Lifesaving) who had rowed to the rescue. 'What are you going to do in the future, Miss Stein?' the *Daily Mirror* enquired. 'I am going to see St Dunstan's through,' she said quietly.[9]

On 16 September 1919, Pearson informed the Committee of the outcome of a visit to Germany by Mrs Myburgh (presumably a representative of St Dunstan's). This was 'with a view to discovering what was being done for the men of the German forces who had been blinded'. The conclusion was that 'the arrangements at St Dunstan's were upon a much wider and sounder basis and that we have nothing to learn from the Institutions of the enemy'. (This was not strictly true. For example, in their provision of guide dogs for the blind, the Germans were more advanced than the British.)

For the duration of the war, and for a short time thereafter, South African athlete and former test cricketer Charles H. Vintcent and his wife Lilian (née Jackson), lived in London. Pearson was delighted when they offered, on their return to South Africa in 1918, to be St Dunstan's representatives on the organization's Aftercare Committee, which had been established in that same year in the city of George, Western Cape.[10] Charles would serve as Chairman and his wife Lilian as Honorary Secretary and the Committee would be instrumental in raising funds in aid of both South African and Rhodesian St Dunstaners.

In November 1919, Pearson was anxious that with the forthcoming repossession of St Dunstan's by Otto Kahn, he would struggle to find sufficient accommodation for the displaced men in other St Dunstan's' properties.[11] However, with the new year came good news, for in January 1920 the NIB, on behalf of St Dunstan's, obtained a lease for nearby St John's Lodge. It had been built in 1812 and since January 1917, it was Sir John Ellerman's Hospital for Disabled Officers, Sir John being a ship owner and financier. This would now become the new headquarters of St Dunstan's.

Meanwhile, the treasurer informed the Committee that the proceeds of a concert given at the Royal Albert Hall on 9 December 1919, featuring English concert and operatic contralto Clara Butt, together with an Empire Ball to be held on 21 January 1920, also at the Royal Albert Hall, would be donated to St Dunstan's Aftercare Fund.[12]

On 20 March 1920 the Committee resolved to create an Estate Office Department 'to facilitate the purchase and renting of houses, shops, poultry-farms, etc. for St Dunstan's men'. Meanwhile, the secretary read a statement 'showing the satisfactory result of St Dunstan's

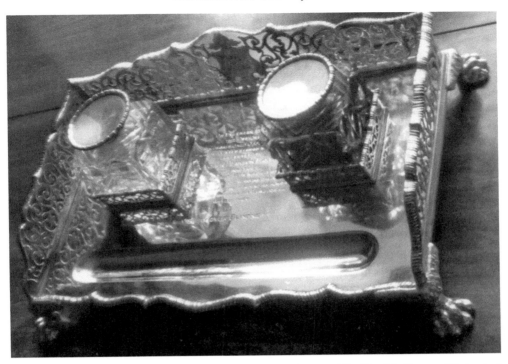

Inkstand presented to Pearson by his St Dunstaners, 15 December 1919. (*The Hon. Mrs Egerton-Warburton*)

Above left: Charles Vintcent, 1930. (*St Dunstan's South Africa*)

Above right: Lilian Vintcent, 1930. (*St Dunstan's South Africa*)

exhibits at the Ideal Home and Industrial Exhibition.[13]

Further good news came on 5 July 1920 when it was announced that a grant of £30,000 had been made to St Dunstan's by the United Services Fund (created to provide financial support to institutions concerned with the welfare of ex-service men and their dependents) towards the upkeep of the Cheltenham Annexe, and the purchase and upkeep of a proposed new annexe at North Berwick in Scotland. On 6 October, Pearson informed the Committee that the Tantallon Hotel in North Berwick, East Lothian, Scotland, had now been acquired as an additional annexe; and that yet another new annexe at St Leonards-on-Sea, Sussex, 'for bedridden men & those physically or mentally incapable of training & who will therefore, need looking after for the rest of their lives,' would probably open within the next two to three weeks.

In 1920, another of St Dunstan's staff was publically honoured when Arnold Lawson received a knighthood. That September he was succeeded by Colonel Reginald E. Bickerton as St Dunstan's consultant ophthalmologist.[14]

On 16 December 1920, Pearson informed the Committee of his recent visit to Buckingham Palace at the request of the King of Denmark 'and of the contribution to St Dunstan's of £2,000 handed to the Chairman [i.e. Pearson] by His Majesty on behalf of himself and the Queen of Denmark'.[15]

On 23 February 1921 the Committee thanked Mrs Irene Fraser for her offer to 'superintend the upkeep of the house and grounds of St John's Lodge, manage the canteen and continue to assist the Chairman in a general capacity'. It also expressed its gratitude to her husband Captain Fraser for offering to continue as Director of the Aftercare Organization.

The plan for St John's Lodge was outlined by Pearson as follows: The ground floor and top floor were to be used as offices for the secretarial, treasury and aftercare departments, and the middle floor was to be occupied by Captain and Mrs Fraser, with the exception of two rooms which were designated for Pearson's use. (Pearson's offer to pay the rent 'was unanimously rejected by the Committee'.)[16]

On 14 March 1921, Pearson had good news to announce. Otto Kahn had agreed for St Dunstan's to 'continue to use the original workshops for instruction in Braille and typewriting and the Bungalow [Annexe] as accommodation for the men until the end of July, on condition that these buildings shall be vacated, and demolished and removed by the 1st of October next.'[17] On 21 October 1921, Kahn, in a further concession, extended the use of certain rooms at the Bungalow Annexe 'for dances, music practice, etc., until January next'.[18]

Some British St Dunstaners

It is both interesting and instructive to examine the lives of some individual St Dunstaners from Britain whose prospects were transformed by St Dunstan's.

Andrew C. Nugee (Lieutenant, 9th Rifle Brigade) was blinded at Hooge, Belgium, in July 1915. Having graduated from St Dunstan's, he studied at Oxford University where he obtained a BA degree. He then took Holy Orders and in 1921 became a Minister of the Church of England. Over the coming years, five more St Dunstaners followed in his wake and became 'men of the cloth'. Two decades later, Nugee returned to St Dunstan's (Church Stretton) as Chaplain.

Thomas Waldin, the son of a Birmingham saddle-tree maker (the saddle tree being the wooden frame upon which leather saddles are constructed), was an apprentice silversmith. On 20 May 1915, twelve days after his 20th birthday, he crossed the Channel as a rifleman with the 8th Rifle Brigade, bound for Ypres in Belgium. During the following six months he would be wounded twice, and also gassed.

On 30 November 1915, the 8th Rifle Brigade moved into trenches at La Brique in the north-east sector of the Salient; less than a week later, while serving on the Front Line ('firing trench'), Waldin and four of his comrades were straddled by two enemy shells, killing one and injuring four.

As one of the four survivors, Waldin was invalided back to 'Blighty', and admitted to the 2nd London General Hospital, Chelsea, under the care of Major Ormond. His right eye had been damaged beyond repair, and despite the best efforts of the medical staff, they were not able to save the sight of his left eye. When he was in the depths of despair, Pearson arrived at his bedside, and the upshot was that he was admitted to St Dunstan's on 25 February 1916.

That spring, Miss Davidson, the then Matron, had an idea that young ladies living in the vicinity might like to take her St Dunstaners for walks in Regent's Park after lunch on Sunday afternoons. Pearson heartily concurred, and as a result, Waldin met Miss Esther Benwell and the two fell in love. They were married at the nearby Victoria Wesleyan Chapel on 26 October 1916.

In December 1916, having completed his ten-month period of training in boot repairing and mat making, Waldin was duly presented, as was the tradition, with his St Dunstan's Badge—with its motif of a flaming torch. This, he said meant as much to him as any of his wartime medals. He was also presented with a silver teapot, inscribed as follows:

RIFLEMAN THOMAS WALDIN
WITH
THE BEST WISHES OF
SIR ARTHUR PEARSON
AND S^T DUNSTAN'S

Above, left & right: Thomas Waldin's badge, as presented to all St Dunstaners on 'graduation'. (*Jean Norman*); Silver teapot presented to Thomas Waldin by Sir Arthur Pearson and St Dunstan's. (*Peter Waldin*)

Left & below: Braille watches belonging to Thomas Waldin.

Working premises were now found for him by St Dunstan's in St John's Wood, and the Aftercare Department provided him with a complete set of tools and leather at cost price. He subsequently made a successful career for himself as a boot-and-shoe repairer and proprietor of a general stores.

In 1919, Thomas and Esther paid a visit to St Dunstan's with their children Peter and Jean, and had their photograph taken by Sister (subsequently Matron) Winifred Boyd-Rochfort. One of Waldin's customers was Alan, the neighbour's son, who remembers him as a cheerful person, who whistled and played merry tunes on his mouth organ. Waldin also had a keen sense of humour. For instance, when Alan set foot on the gravel path which led up to the shop, Waldin would immediately recognize the boy's footsteps, and gently tease him by singing 'On the Banks of Allan Water'. Then, without being asked, he would weigh out and hand over a quarter pound of 'liquorice laces'—which were Alan's favourite—in a little brown paper bag, in exchange for tuppence.

Angus Buchanan, of Scottish descent and son of a doctor, was from Coleford in

Above: A family visit to St Dunstan's in 1919. *Left to right:* Mrs Benwell, baby Jean Waldin, Thomas Waldin, Peter Waldin, and Thomas's wife Esther. Photograph taken by Sister Winifred Boyd-Rochfort. (*Peter Waldin*)

Right: Thomas Waldin at work in his shop at St John's Wood, 1920. (*Jean Norman*)

Gloucestershire's Forest of Dean. In 1913 he became an undergraduate at Jesus College, Oxford, to which he had won a scholarship in Classics.

When war broke out, he was commissioned into the 4th Battalion, South Wales Borderers. He served in the Gallipoli Campaign and was wounded on 7 August 1915 at Sulva Bay. For his action at Cape Helles on 7 January 1916 he was awarded the Military Cross (MC). Buchanan subsequently served in Mesopotamia, where, during action at the Falauyah Lines on 5 April 1916, he was awarded the VC. The citation reads as follows:

During an attack an officer was lying out in the open severely wounded about 150 yards from cover. Two men went to his assistance and one of them was hit at once. Captain Buchanan, on seeing this, immediately went out and, with the help of the other man, carried the wounded officer to cover under heavy machine gun fire. He then returned and brought in the wounded man, again under heavy fire.[1]

Angus Buchanan VC, at a St Dunstaners' reunion. (*Blind Veterans UK*)

In July 1916 Buchanan was awarded the Russian Imperial Order of St Vladimir, 4th Class (with Swords). On 13 February 1917 he sustained a gunshot wound to the head and was evacuated to India, where he suffered the added complication of malaria. Finally, on 1 June 1917, he returned to England and the following month was admitted to the 2nd London General Hospital, by which time he had lost sight in both of his eyes.

On 8 November 1917, at Bristol, Buchanan was invested with both the VC and the MC by the King. On 20 November 1917, he was admitted to St Dunstan's and remained there until 11 June 1918, when he graduated and returned to Jesus College to resume his studies. He also rowed in the college four. In October 1921 he obtained his degree, and in the following year, successfully passed the Law Society examination. Having been articled to an Oxford firm of lawyers he was admitted, in February 1929, as a solicitor and went into practice in his home village of Coleford. His favourite hobbies were walking, fishing, and (despite his blindness) golf. At his request, funds raised in recognition of his bravery were used to provide a recreation ground for the use of the children of Coleford. It was named after him in his honour.[2]

Edward Murnock Brockie served with the 4th Battalion (City of Aberdeen) Territorial Force, Gordon Highlanders. On 23 February 1916 the 4th Gordons joined 154 Brigade, 51st Highland Division. The first major action in which the 4th Gordons participated was at High Wood from 19–25 July 1916, during the early days of the Battle of the Somme. The British, who occupied about a third of the wood, were attempting to strengthen their defensive position, situated at the apex of a salient. According to the regimental diary, at 1.30 a.m. on the 23rd July 1916, 'our artillery [barrage] lifted and the whole Battn advanced in lines of Coys [Companies]….'

For several reasons the attack 'utterly failed': The Gordons, together with the 9th Royal Scots, were advancing in the face of a German artillery barrage; barbed wire protecting the enemy trenches remained uncut; it was dark, and the ground was 'so broken up with shell holes that in a few minutes all sense of direction was more or less lost'; there were fallen trees and undergrowth to contend with; and there had been no opportunity for reconnaissance. Casualties were 'very heavy, and included 12 officers and about 250 other ranks, of whom Private Brockie was one. Brockie was blinded, but precisely how is not known.[3]

At St Dunstan's, Brockie 'trained in mat making and attained a very good standard of workmanship and sold the articles that he made locally.[4]

Frederick ('Bill') le Gros Clark was blinded and lost his right hand in an 'accident with a bomb' while he was in camp at New Barracks, Gosport, Hampshire. This was on 11 November 1918, the very last day of the First World War. Nevertheless, he became a writer—of short stories, children's stories, and novels—journalist, and pamphleteer, and a distinguished activist in the field of research into the social sciences. He was also concerned with the welfare of the blind, not only in the UK but elsewhere, including in the Soviet Union. He later developed an interest in health and nutrition and worked for the United Nations Food and Agriculture Organization.

Some St Dunstaners from Overseas

Of the service personnel from overseas who were blinded during the First World War, about half were evacuated to the United Kingdom, where the expectation was that the 'Mother Country' would look after them in return for their service and sacrifice. Pearson, in offering to admit them to St Dunstan's for rehabilitation and training—an offer which was almost invariably accepted—ensured that this expectation was amply and generously fulfilled.

Canadians

Seventy or so Canadian service personnel were admitted to St Dunstan's, one of whom was Alexander Griswold Viets (Lance-corporal, Princess Patricia's Canadian Light Infantry—PPCLI), a bookkeeper from Digby, Nova Scotia, who had previously served in the 3rd Battalion Canadian Mounted Rifles. At Ypres, in May 1915, Viets was repairing a trench when he was blinded by an exploding mortar bomb. When he returned to Canada from St Dunstan's, he was the first war-blinded Canadian soldier to do so. Having graduated from St Dunstan's, he returned home and resumed work as a salesman for his former employer, the Imperial Life Assurance Company of Canada.

Edwin Albert Baker MC (Lieutenant, 6th Field Company, Royal Canadian Engineers) was an electrical engineer from Kingston, Ontario, and a graduate in electrical engineering from that city's Queen's University. Prior to the First World War, he had served for a year in the 4th Canadian Hussars and for four years in the 5th Field Company, Canadian Engineers.

On 10 October 1915, Baker was blinded at Kemmel in Belgium 'by a rifle bullet which entered the right side of the orbit, passing through the left globe and then to the right'.[1] He arrived at St Dunstan's on 2 January 1916 and was discharged in July. On his return home he found employment in Toronto as a typist with the Ontario Hydro-Electric Power Commission (which was concerned with the harnessing of power from Niagara Falls).

In 1918, together with six other Canadians, one of whom was Viets, Baker founded the CNIB which established around fifty offices across Canada from coast to coast. Baker and Viets also joined the Board of Directors of Toronto's Free Library of Braille Literature, and were instrumental in expanding its facilities.

Baker served as Vice-President of the CNIB's first National Council; oversaw the Aftercare and Training programme for blinded Canadian servicemen, and in 1920, became the organization's general secretary (until 1962).

Edwin Baker seated second from left with fellow Canadians; Ian Fraser to his left. (*Blind Veterans UK*)

He sponsored ophthalmic surveys and medical aid for native Canadians in the far north, helped organize the first mass survey of school children in Toronto, which led to the establishment of classes for people with vision loss, and oversaw the first national survey of the incidence and causes of vision loss in Canada.

Baker's interests extended far beyond his own organization. He served as president of the World Council for the Welfare of the Blind [now known as the World Blind Union] for three terms, and was, for many years, the only lay member of the Canadian Ophthalmological Society. He was a member of the National Advisory Council on the Rehabilitation of Disabled Persons for 10 years and was involved in the formation of the Royal Commonwealth Society for the Blind in London, England.[2]

Baker also became a leading light in various war veterans' associations.[3]

Harris Turner (Private, PPCLI) was a newspaper reporter from Saskatoon, Saskatchewan. At Sanctuary Wood, Belgium on 2 June 1916, he was blinded after being 'hit by flying pieces of shrapnel in both eyes … while resisting an attack'.[4] He was subsequently admitted first to the Military Hospital, Edmonton, Middlesex, and then to the Royal London Eye Hospital, Moorfields, prior to arriving at St Dunstan's on 25 November 1916.

On his return to Canada, Turner became a member of the Saskatchewan Legislature, where he put to good use the debating skills he had learned at St Dunstan's. He went on to found his own newspaper, *Turner's Weekly*.[5]

Walter (sometimes known as William, and 'Bill' to his friends) Chester Dies (Private, 50th Battalion, Canadian Infantry) was a clerk from Toronto. In February 1917 he was blinded at

Charles Clarence Henry Miller and VAD Sullivan, 1917. (*Blind Veterans UK*)

Vimy, France, by an enemy grenade. He also lost his right arm. After St Dunstan's he returned home and established his own tobacco and stationery shop. In November 1919 he married Grace Price, by whom he had two sons. Dies took a keen interest in the newly formed CNIB, and subsequently became a member of its National Council. In 1922 he was a founder member of the Sir Arthur Pearson Club of Soldiers and Sailors, of which he became president on four separate occasions between 1923 and 1961.

Thomas Edwin Perrett (Lieutenant Colonel, 68th Battalion, Canadian Expeditionary Force), married to Jessie, was a teacher from Regina, Saskatchewan. Prior to the war, he had served in the 95th Saskatchewan Rifles. Perrett was blinded at Ypres on 30 September 1917. After St Dunstan's he returned to Regina to take up his former post as Head of the Regina Normal School Teacher Training College.

In January 1919, as already mentioned, Pearson paid a visit to the CNIB's headquarters in Toronto. Here, he was entertained at Pearson Hall (so named in his honour) by twenty-five 'graduates' of St Dunstan's, including Viets and Baker. 'We have but carried our torches from St Dunstan's, where they were lit,' declared Baker (the incumbent CNIB vice-president) on that occasion.[6]

Pearson regretted that having visited Canada, he did not have the time to pay similar visits to Australia, New Zealand, and South Africa.

Charles Clarence Henry Miller was admitted to St Dunstan's on 4 June 1917. His life had been, and would be, far from straightforward. Born in Aberdeen on 11 June 1883, Miller spent his early life in the USA and Canada, and from 1909 to 1913, he served in the US Navy. On 26 June 1916 at Toronto, he enlisted as a private soldier in the 173rd Battalion, Canadian

Highlanders, Canadian Expeditionary Force. He was thirty-three years old, single, and an electrician, and his current place of residence was Minersville, Pennsylvania, USA. According to St Dunstan's records, Miller was wounded in France on 11 June 1916. The truth, however, was somewhat different—Miller had never actually set foot in that country.

Miller's battalion arrived in England on 20 November 1916, and its men billeted at Bramshott Camp, near Aldershot in Hampshire. However, on 24 February 1917, Miller was admitted to hospital at Bramshott for a period of several weeks having experienced problems with his right eye, which was said to be 'affected with old Iritis and Choroiditis'. Meanwhile, at about this time, he married Margaret Williams, at East Preston, Sussex.

On 4 June 1917, Miller was admitted to St Dunstan's. Three days later he was admitted to the 2nd Eastern General Hospital, Brighton, and in that same month, according to him, his right eye was removed (enucleated) at the Middlesex Hospital, London. Having returned to St Dunstan's, he was transferred on 28 August 1917 to that organization's Brighton branch, and discharged on 18 December.

On 21 December 1917, Miller was admitted to Ontario Military Hospital in Orpington, Kent. From here, he was sent to the Lord Derby War Hospital at Warrington, Lancashire. He was now suffering from 'melancholia with delusions', and had attempted to commit suicide 'by taking Nitrate of silver solution.'

> He was charged with malingering in the Hospital by feigning blindness and while awaiting trial cried and threatened to end his life by throwing himself under cars.... He quickly recovered when charge was dismissed on ground of mental irresponsibility.

Finally, on 15 April 1918, Miller was invalided back to Canada. At the Queen's Military Hospital, Kingston, Ontario, it was stated that Miller was a 'Mental case' who

> tells different stories each day about date of enlistment, about his service. Says he was in France and was wounded in eye and abdomen whereas he never got further than England. His stories apparently are for the purpose of gaining sympathy and assistance and imposing on people.

It was decided that he should therefore 'be placed in an Institution for his mental condition'. Miller died on 29 June 1946, presumably in a psychiatric institution.[7]

What is to be deduced from Miller's story? This was a man who had served in both the US Navy and the Canadian Army, and whose character, while in the service, was described as 'very good'. So how may his sudden change of personality, coupled with his blindness, be explained?

Choroiditis and iritis may both be signs of a syphilitic infection. Furthermore, the latter stages of syphilis may be characterized by mental deterioration, depression, and delusions. It is therefore likely that he had contracted syphilis as a younger man, and that this was the cause of his condition. Were his doctors aware that this might be the case? If so, there is no mention of it in the medical notes.

Miller is therefore deserving of sympathy, rather than censure. And if, in order to gain admission to St Dunstan's—which catered specifically for those who had been blinded in war—he concocted the story about his being blinded while on active service, then who can blame him?

Australians

Seventy-five or so Australian service personnel were admitted to St Dunstan's. New Zealand-born James ('Jim') T. S. Scrymgeour (Private, 2nd Australian Light Horse) was the son of a sheep farmer from Queensland. In July 1918 he was blinded while serving in Palestine, and invalided back to Brisbane as a 'cot-case' (a person who is too ill to leave their bed).

On 25 November 1918, Scrymgeour married expert horsewoman Helen Marjorie Brown. In 1919 the couple travelled to Britain and in October, Scrymgeour was admitted to St Dunstan's. On their return home to Queensland, the Scrymgeours settled at Netherby in Warwick, a property owned by Jim's father, William. Here, they established the Netherby Shorthorn Stud, using lines of cattle previously imported by William. In order to find his way around the buildings and stables on his farm, Scrymgeour adopted the system of guide-wires, used at St Dunstan's for athletics events. In 1930, Scrymgeour's bull 'Netherby Royal Challenge' won the first of six championships at the Royal National Show, Brisbane.

In 1937, Scrymgeour converted to a different breed, Poll Shorthorn, and with equal success,

Jim Scrymgeour and his wife Marjorie, at Netherby Shorthorn Stud, Warwick, Queensland, parading their champion bull 'Netherby Royal Challenge'. The animal won the Grand Champion Bull Award from 1931 to 1935 at the Brisbane Royal Show. (The Land, *North Richmond, NSW, Australia*)

winning won thirteen senior championships at the Royal Easter Show, Sydney, between 1939 and 1955. From 1938–56, Scrymgeour served on the council of the Poll Shorthorn Society of Australasia,[8] and in 1954 he was awarded the OBE for his services to the cattle industry in Australia. He wrote several books, including *The Blind Cattlemen*.

Dudley A. Tregent (Sergeant, 3rd Division, 107th Field Artillery [Howitzer] Battery) served for almost three years on the Western Front; on 17 October 1918, the month prior to the signing of the Armistice, he was wounded by an enemy shell and lost the sight in both his eyes. Only five days prior to this date he had been promoted to the rank of Sergeant.

While receiving treatment for his wounds at the 2nd London General Hospital, Chelsea, Tregent was visited by staff from St Dunstan's, and then on 15 November 1918, Pearson himself came to see him. When he had recovered sufficiently, Tregent was granted permission to travel to Newport in Wales where his brother Percy (Private, 59th Infantry Battalion), who had also been wounded during the successful assault on Mont St Quentin and Peronne, was convalescing.

> Dudley was greatly concerned as to what he could make of his life. He told Percy that he was not going to sell matches in the street. After a long discussion between the two brothers, they came to the conclusion that as Dudley's education qualified him for entry into a university, he should approach Melbourne University with a view to embarking upon a Law course, that being his ambition.[9]

Meanwhile, having accepted the Chief's invitation, Tregent was admitted to St Dunstan's on 11 December 1918, and sent from there temporarily to West House, Brighton, for further convalescence. He returned to St Dunstan's shortly afterwards.

> [Tregent] being of a studious nature did not indulge in all the hostel's activities but devoted all time possible to reading serious books for which purpose he became adept at enlisting readers amongst the attractive V.A.D.'s, one of whom he subsequently married.[10]

The lady in question was Eileen Sharp. Eileen was born in Scotland, and when she was aged four she and her family emigrated to New York City, USA. Having trained as a nurse she volunteered, in 1915, to work at St Dunstan's as a VAD and it was at the College Annexe where she and Tregent met and fell in love. Meanwhile, Tregent 'was taken for a time to a college in Cambridge, where he continued preparations for the university course in Law, on which he had set his mind.'[11]

On 26 June 1919, having passed his Braille reading and writing tests and his typewriting test, Tregent had a discussion with the Chief whereupon lessons in both English and French were arranged for him to commence after the summer holidays, for which the required reading matter would be provided in Braille. Along with the mental stimulation, Tregent's physical health and strength improved: he was a keen walker: 'it was no trouble for him to 'circumnavigate' Regent's Park—a distance of about four miles.'[12]

Eileen Sharp and Dudley Tregent were married in London on 12 July 1920 and the couple went to live in Australia. Having become the first blind student to enrol at and graduate from Melbourne University's Law School (LLB and Master of Laws, both with honours), Tregent

Above left: Dudley Tregent before he was blinded. (*Eileen Crewes*)

Above right: Dudley Tregent and Eileen Sharp on their wedding day, 12 July 1920. (*Eileen Crewes*)

Below: Dudley Tregent at St Dunstan's. (*Eileen Crewes*)

subsequently embarked upon a successful career as a solicitor. He also became the Legacy Club of Melbourne's first honorary solicitor; the club's objective was to assist with the care and welfare of the dependents of deceased servicemen.[13]

Elmer 'Sticky' Glew (Private, 8th Infantry Battalion) was wounded in the landings at the Dardanelles in April 1915, and Charles Henry Hills (Staff Sergeant, 2nd Australian Field Ambulance) was blinded at Gallipoli on 7 June 1915. Both Glew and Hills arrived at St Dunstan's in August 1915, where the former trained in massage and the latter in poultry farming. On their return home, Glew and Hills founded aftercare services ('Committees') for the returning war blinded—Glew in Victoria, and Hills in New South Wales—with the assistance of the Australian Red Cross. Soon, every Australian state was able to boast a similar facility.[14]

At St Dunstan's, bonds were forged between the men which often flourished and led to great things after their graduation.

> Great friendships had formed among those who had been sent to that great institution....
> Upon their return to the shores of Australia and their home, these friendships were greatly missed and so it was agreed that they form themselves into associations for their mutual help and advancement.[15]

In other words, the comradeship of their fellow blinded servicemen was what the men valued so highly, and placed such great store upon.

In 1921, in Melbourne, Victoria, the Association of Blinded Soldiers of Australia (ABSA)

Elmer Glew. (*Vision Australia Heritage Collection*)

was founded. The war blinded were also cared for and trained at the Royal Victorian Institute for the Blind in Melbourne and at the Royal Blind Society in Sydney.

New Zealanders

The first New Zealander to be blinded during the First World War was Sergeant William Trickey Woods of the Otage Battalion, New Zealand Expeditionary Force (NZEF), Otago Infantry Battalion, on 10 May 1915 at Cape Helles in the Dardanelles. At St Dunstan's he learned physiotherapy, and on his return home in 1916, he worked in the service of the government before setting up in private practice in Christchurch.[16]

When the plight of New Zealand's war-blinded—numbering twenty-eight by the end of the war[17]—came to the notice of that country's Commercial Travellers' and Warehousemen's Association, it responded by setting up various branches throughout the country to raise funds and assist the men, most of whom, if not all, had been admitted to St Dunstan's. The War Funds Committee of Wellington was also established during the First World War, with affiliated Associations in Auckland, Canterbury, and Otago. From this fund the sum of £500 was donated to St Dunstan's in recognition of the help afforded to New Zealanders blinded in the war.

James ('Jim') Chisholm (Rifleman, 3rd Battalion, New Zealand Rifle Brigade—NZRB) was born in Scotland and worked for twelve years in London as a blacksmith before emigrating to New Zealand in 1903. In 1907 he married his cousin Isabella (née Chisholm) but became a widower in 1910 when she died due to complications in pregnancy.

[Since 1904] Chisholm worked as a gum digger [extracting gum from kauri trees, to be crafted into items of jewellery or decoration] in Northland and leased 2 acres of land in the Houhora area at Waihopo [North Island] to grow potatoes and keep hens.

In 1915, at the age of 38, Chisholm entrusted his potatoes and poultry to a friend for safekeeping, his hoard of gum to the Government and travelled south to Trentham to enlist.

On 15 September 1916, Chisholm was wounded and blinded in the Battle of Fleurs-Courcelette by shrapnel from an exploding enemy shell. To compound the tragedy, Chisholm's mother Walterina had died only the day previously at her home in Skirling, Peebleshire, Scotland. On 26 September he was admitted to the 2nd London General Hospital, Chelsea.[18]

On 26 January 1917, after four months of convalescence, Chisholm was admitted to St Dunstan's, but immediately granted three weeks leave so that he might visit his family at Skirling. Meanwhile, in his poem 'The Little Iron Shanty', he dreamed of his adoptive home.

> There's a little iron shanty, in New Zealand's far, far north,
> And oh! I am longing to be there.
> The contents of that shanty are not much in money's worth
> For of furniture I even have no chair.
> But I love my little shanty and I'm longing to be there

James Chisholm beside
one of his home-made
huts on the gumfield,
Northland, New Zealand,
prior to the First World
War. (*Alison Jones*)

Though my table's made of boxes and a meat case is my chair.
But the sun shines there so splendid and the weather is so warm
And I could walk about all day and not take any harm.

Oh! Take me to my old friends, the digger and his dog
Away from this cold climate, away from London fog.
In the land of glorious sunshine and the beauteous Christmas Tree,
And my little iron shanty, hard by the Tasman Sea.[19]

['Digger'—a colloquial term for an Australian or New Zealander.]

Having trained in poultry farming at St Dunstan's, Chisholm returned to New Zealand on
21 November 1917. In early May 1918, Chisholm was joined in New Zealand by his father
Walter, younger brother Walter (junior) who was deaf, and sister Jean, who had decided to
set up home there also and assist James in his endeavours—i.e. to become a poultryman
and to establish a tropical orchard. To this end, with typical thoroughness, St Dunstan's
had arranged for Jean also, prior to emigrating, to undergo a course of training in poultry
farming at Sutton Coldfield in the English Midlands. Said Jean, in reference to James and
Walter (junior) respectively, 'I am the eyes of the blind and the ears of the deaf'.[20]

Pearson and St Dunstan's were never far from Chisholm's thoughts, as another poem of his,
'St Dunstan's', which contains a clear allusion to the Chief, reveals:

When nets of war had made us blind
The gods to us were more than kind
They sought around and soon did find,
St Dunstan's for our Home.

A blind man took a leading part
He knew the game and taught the art
We'll sing this song from ev'ry heart,
St Dunstan's is our Home.

Though living now where e'eer we please
In corners of the seven seas
We sing this song to ev'ry breeze,
St Dunstan's is our Home.[21]

Donald McPhee (Sergeant, 2nd Battalion NZRB), formerly a farmer, enlisted in May 1915 and rose steadily through the ranks. During the opening phase of the Battle of Messines, Belgium, which commenced on 7 June 1917, he was wounded in the face by shrapnel and thus blinded.

After treatment at various hospitals in France, McPhee finally arrived at St Dunstan's on 13 October 1917. Two years later, in October 1919, he returned home to New Zealand where he became a practising masseur. He also presided over Auckland's Social Club for the Blind.[22] In 1940, he was appointed by the government as a member of the Physiotherapy Advisory Committee to the Medical Committee in connection with the New Zealand Army Physiotherapy Services.[23]

On 14 August 1914, just ten days after the outbreak of war, Sir Thomas Mackenzie, a former prime minister of New Zealand and that country's High Commissioner in London from 1912 to 1920, convened a meeting of expatriate New Zealanders living in London. The outcome was that the New Zealand War Contingent Association (NZWCA) was formed, with himself as Chairman.[24] Its aim was to assist New Zealand's servicemen by 'providing them with comforts, visiting them in hospital, securing accommodation for convalescents after they had passed through the hospitals… also by keeping in touch with the soldiers and their relatives'.[25]

This, it was hoped, would also serve to maintain morale. At that time, Sir Thomas could not have guessed at the tragedy which was shortly to befall his son Clutha N. Mackenzie, nor that the latter would subsequently have a pivotal role to play in the activities of the NZWCA.

Having studied at agricultural college, Clutha Mackenzie (Trooper, Wellington Mounted Rifles) was employed on a sheep farm prior to the war. He served in Egypt and subsequently at Gallipoli, where, on 12 August 1915, during the aftermath of the disastrous attack at Chanuk Bair and Hill 60, he was wounded in the face by shrapnel and blinded.

Mackenzie was evacuated via Alexandria to the UK, where he was treated for three months at the New Zealand War Contingent Hospital at Walton-on-Thames, Surrey. In the second week of November 1915, he was admitted to St Dunstan's where he became proficient in Braille and typewriting. These skills stood him in good stead later when he became editor of the *Chronicles of the NZEF*—a periodical newspaper published fortnightly by the NZWCA. Pearson was quick to recognize the importance of the *Chronicles*, and he accordingly granted Mackenzie an extended stay at St Dunstan's; the New Zealander ended up in the editor's chair for almost four years. Having graduated from St Dunstan's, Mackenzie was offered accommodation at 21 Portland Place, where Pearson and the officers had their quarters (even though he was not an officer himself). As for the *Chronicles*, its office was located at No. 11 Southampton Row (the New Zealand Military Headquarters being situated nearby at No. 8).

The first issue of the *Chronicles* appeared on 30 August 1916, and the initial print run was 1,500 copies, each of which were normally priced 6*d*, but 3*d* to troops. Patients in hospital received their copies free of charge. The magazine was disseminated to New Zealand service personnel in all theatres of war in which they were operating, including Gallipoli, the Western Front, and the Middle East and also, of course, to the home country.

The *Chronicles* published accounts of the state of health and progress of wounded New Zealanders—including those who had been blinded—together with details of those who had been killed in action, died of wounds, or were missing. Whatever information that could be gleaned as to the fate of New Zealand prisoners of war in Germany and Turkey was also published in the *Chronicles*. (It should be remembered that out of a total population of about 1 million, 103,000—or in excess of 10 per cent—served, of whom about 60 per cent were either killed or wounded.)

St Dunstan's Blinded Services Association of New Zealand, AGM, 1961. Front row, from left: Donald ('Don') McPhee OBE, James ('Jim') May MBE, Sir Clutha Mackenzie.

The *Chronicles* contained first-hand accounts by servicemen of life at the Front (which were of course subject to censorship by the military authorities), editorials, articles by British and New Zealand war correspondents, reports about rugby football, soccer, hockey, golf, and boxing matches between NZEF units and those from other countries, poems and cartoons composed by the men, and of course, messages of goodwill and enquiries from loved ones back in the home country. They also provided information about how money raised in New Zealand to support the troops was being spent.

In May to September 1917, Mackenzie returned to New Zealand, during which time Lance Corporal A. L. Williams[26] became acting editor.

His tour of New Zealand in 1917 seemed to have captured the imagination of the people. As the guest of honour at various public meetings and civic receptions his achievements and courage were lauded.[27]

In December 1917, Mackenzie spent four days at the Ypres sector of the Western Front. It was said that he was

pivotal in setting up the *Chronicles* and ensuring their ongoing success, with his influential family connections, his drive and commitment to their continued publication, and the written contributions he made in editorials and opinion pieces.

The editor… was central to the *Chronicles* achieving their purpose. He was deeply involved in every aspect of their production including funding, writing (not just editorials), editing, printing and distribution. His leadership motivated the small editorial team, which he kept together even after their offices were bombed, destroying material which was being prepared for publication.[28]

Mackenzie himself was generous in his praise of both his father Sir Thomas and Pearson. In this endeavour, he said, they 'gave their warm support and I always remain grateful'.[29] However, as the war progressed, it was noticeable how Mackenzie's writings, and those of the war correspondents and servicemen, became more sanguine as the full horror of life—and death—at the Front became more and more apparent.

In total, sixty-one issues of the *Chronicle of the NZEF* were published, with the final edition coming out in January 1919. Mackenzie's achievement to manage and coordinate a periodical on which his servicemen comrades and their families and friends on the other side of the world came to depend, is truly remarkable. Furthermore, in creating the *Chronicles*, Mackenzie blazed the trail for St Dunstan's own periodical magazine—the *St Dunstan's Review*.

In February 1919, his task as editor of the *Chronicles* completed, Mackenzie finally sailed for home. He later reflected movingly on those extraordinary times.

My thoughts wander back to that rough, dear old sheep-station, and to my mate, who rode away with me that day, and who fell nine months later leading his company in a gallant charge on strong Turkish positions at Cape Helles; but I am not sad, for we are both happy and he is not so far away. Then my thoughts return from those irresponsible days among those sunlit peaceful hills, and I contemplate myself, an autocratic editor in the turmoil of London, dictating to thousands his views on this and that. And blind, too! How strange! I chuckle, and wonder when I shall wake from my reverie to find myself, tired after a long day's mustering, wandering homewards in the gloaming, asleep on my horse's back.[30]

In July 1919, Pearson got in touch with Mackenzie again:

Sir Arthur Pearson has requested me to take charge of the New Zealand blind soldiers who were at St Dunstan's Hospital for the Blind, in regard to their future welfare. There are about a couple of dozen of them—a really fine lot of men—about half of whom have come back. The rest are still at St Dunstan's.[31]

In October 1919, Mackenzie married Doris Sawyer, a VAD whom he had met at St Dunstan's. (He had proposed marriage to Doris by cable from Bombay while *en route* to New Zealand in early 1919.)

In 1921, Mackenzie was elected to New Zealand's parliamentary House of Representatives. Further challenges now awaited him: From 1923 (until 1938) he served as director of New Zealand's Jubilee Institute for the Blind (later the New Zealand Institute for the Blind) at Auckland. As a result of fundraising, in which he played an important role,[32] workshops for the blind were built in Auckland, together with a hostel—a handsome brick building with a Doric-style colonnade. It opened in 1926 and was named 'Pearson House'. In 1935, Mackenzie was knighted for his services to the blind.

South Africans

Forty-two South African service personnel were blinded, of whom about half were admitted to St Dunstan's. On their return to South Africa, they relied for help and advice on St Dunstan's South Africa Committee and its leading lights, Charles H. Vintcent and his wife Lilian. The men were also assisted by philanthropically minded individuals and by the religious community until Durban lawyer John Edward Palmer founded the Association for the Blind and started a fund for them.

Since the outbreak of war, Robert W. ('Mike') Bowen (Sergeant, 2nd South African Infantry) had served first in South-West Africa and then in France. On 19 September 1917, Bowen was in the vicinity of Ypres, and received orders that the following day he and his men were to go 'over the top'.

In the ensuing battle on 20 September, Bowen and four of his comrades were forced to take cover in a shell crater. One of their number was Hugh Arthur Stayt (Private, also 2nd South African Infantry). Stayt had left his rifle in another refuge about 30 yards away which he and others had recently been occupying, so he decided to return to collect it. As he was doing so he heard the whine of a shell, and when it exploded he realized that his comrades in the shell crater had been hit. In fact, three were dead with two wounded. Bowen 'had a bad gash across his eyes. It was evident then that his sight had been destroyed and that he had other very severe wounds.'

Stayt now helped Bowen (who was the first South African soldier to be blinded in the First World War) and the other man to the shelter of a concrete pillbox. Just a few hours later, on that same day, and by a ghastly coincidence, Stayt himself was blinded by a sniper's bullet. He was aged seventeen. Both men were evacuated to England to the 2nd London General Hospital. From here, they were admitted to St Dunstan's—Stayt on 21 January 1918 and Bowen on 27 February 1918.

Having graduated from St Dunstan's, Bowen obtained a degree in law at Cambridge University and in 1920 was called to the Bar in London. In 1922 he married New Zealander Eleanor Gillies, sister of the famous plastic surgeon Harold Gillies; she was living with her grandmother in England. The two had met at the 2nd London General Hospital, where Eleanor worked as a VAD. In the same year Bowen returned to South Africa with his new wife, joined the South African Bar, and embarked on what was to be a distinguished career as an advocate. Seven years later he became a member of the South African Parliament. He was a leading light in the founding of the South African National Council for the Blind, of which he became its first chairman in 1929.

Hugh Stayt trained at St Dunstan's as a poultry farmer. The challenges—not to say prejudice and discrimination—which he subsequently faced were to test his determination to the full. Having returned home to South Africa in May 1919, he commenced poultry farming

Above left: Robert Bowen in the 1920s. (*St Dunstan's South Africa*)

Above right: Hugh Stayt in the 1920s. (*St Dunstan's South Africa*)

at Pietermaritzburg, Natal. However, the venture was not a success. In June 1921 he returned to England to marry Evelyn Dyson, a St Dunstan's VAD and the daughter of Sir Frank Dyson, the Astronomer Royal.

In 1923, Stayt returned again to England to study anthropology at Cambridge University, in which subject he achieved a First Class Honours Degree. Having returned to South Africa he applied for the post of Professor of Anthropology at Cape Town University, but was rejected on the grounds that as a blind man he would not be able to deal with the administrative work. However, he went on to study for a PhD at the university, the subject of his thesis being the Bavenda (or Venda) people of the Northern Transvaal. The thesis was published in book form in 1931 by Oxford University Press.

Sadly, Stayt was unable to obtain an academic post. He therefore returned to England and qualified in physiotherapy. He subsequently set up in practice in Cape Town with fellow St Dunstaner Alex Kirstein (who had been blinded in German West Africa in May 1915). Misfortune struck again, however, when Kirstein relocated to Rhodesia, whereupon the partnership was dissolved.

Stayt now returned to England where he obtained a doctorate in osteopathy. In 1936 he returned yet again to South Africa, and set up in practice as an osteopath in Natal's coastal resort of Port Shepstone.

With the advent of the Second World War, Stayt obtained a commission as Recruiting Officer of the South African Defence Force for the South Coast District of Natal, with the rank of Captain.[33]

Indians

In India, practical difficulties such as diversity of languages and the vastness of the country precluded the founding of a St Dunstan's-style training establishment. However, St Dunstan's donated a lump sum to the Indian Soldiers Board, out of which 5 rupees per month for life was paid to every Indian blinded in the war, in addition to his pension.[34] In 1919, St Dunstaner the Reverend W. Gilbert Speight (Yorks & Lancs Regiment), blinded at Doesinghe, Belgium in 1915, was appointed to the post of Director of the Palmacottah School for the Blind in Southern India. His work for blind children (of all races and creeds) became so well known and admired that similar institutions sprung up all over the subcontinent.[35]

Pearson and Helen Keller

It was a series of extraordinary coincidences that brought together two of the most pre-eminent people in the world of the blind: Arthur Pearson of Britain and Helen Keller of the USA. This began on 7 May 1915 with the torpedoing, off the coast of Ireland (by a German U-boat), of the British Cunard passenger liner *Lusitania*. Of the 1,959 passengers and crew aboard, only 761 survived (128 Americans were lost from a total of 197).

Travelling on the *Lusitania*, which was *en route* from New York to Liverpool, was George Kessler—otherwise known as the 'Champagne King'—who owned a wine-importing company in New York City. Kessler also had a home in England on the banks of the Thames at Bourne End, Hertfordshire—the same village in which Arthur Pearson had his home. In fact, it appears that the two already knew each other for this reason.

Kessler was thrown into the water when the torpedo struck; he managed to get into a lifeboat, but by the time he was rescued, only three of its twelve occupants remained alive. While recovering in hospital in England, Kessler was visited by Pearson who told him about St Dunstan's.

In the light of this near-death experience and bearing what Pearson had told him, Kessler resolved to devote himself to helping servicemen blinded in the war. To this end, on 11 November 1915, he and his wife Cora formally organized the British, French, and Belgian Permanent Blind Relief War Fund in Paris, with French war veteran George Raverat as head of European Operations. Finally, having returned to the USA, the Kesslers enlisted the help of the legendary Helen Adams Keller, then aged thirty-five, whose name was known throughout the world. Helen readily agreed to help, telling Kessler,

My heart glows every time I think of what you are doing for the blinded soldiers. May our work grow until every man who has given his sight for his country will feel the comforting warmth of a friendly hand guiding him through a dark, strange world.[1]

Helen was born in Tuscumbia, Alabama, on 27 June 1880, the daughter of Captain Arthur Henley Keller—who had fought in the Confederate Army during the American Civil War—and his wife Kate Adams Keller. Tragedy quickly struck Helen, for at the age of only nineteen months she became not only blind, but also deaf. This is believed to have been caused either by scarlet fever or by meningitis. She became increasingly aggressive, destructive, and unmanageable: a classic example of someone who finds themselves being looked after by a family, who through no fault of their own, lacked the skills to help her. She also felt isolated from her peers, with whom there was no communication.

Helen Adams Keller. (*Courtesy of Vision Australia Heritage Collection*)

Fortunately for Helen, her mother had read Charles Dickens's *American Notes for General Circulation* (published in 1842, following that author's five-month visit to the USA). In it, Dickens describes the help and education that had been given to another blind and deaf child, Laura Bridgman of Hanover, New Hampshire, by a Dr Samuel Gridley Howe. The problem was, however, that Dr Howe was now deceased.

Helen was about six years old when her father learnt of a Dr Julian John Chisholm, an 'eminent oculist in Baltimore [Maryland] who had been successful in many cases that had seemed hopeless'.[2] Chisholm was unable to assist, but recommended to them Dr Alexander Graham Bell, inventor of the telephone, who had chosen to devote himself to the teaching of the blind. Bell, in turn, advised the Kellers to approach Michael Anagnos, Director of the Perkins Institute for the Blind in Boston, Massachusetts, where the late Dr Howe had previously worked.

The outcome was that on 3 March 1887—shortly before her seventh birthday—Helen was introduced to the person who would transform her life: Anne Mansfield Sullivan, a former pupil of the Institute who was herself partially sighted. Anne would become Helen's tutor.

Anne taught Helen Braille, and in May 1888, the latter enrolled at the Perkins Institute where she met other blind children who 'were so happy and contented that I lost all sense of pain in the pleasure of their companionship'.[3]

In the spring of 1890, a Mrs Lamson, who had been one of Laura Bridgman's teachers, recommended that Helen consult Miss Sarah Fuller, Principal of the Horace Mann School for the Deaf in Allston, Massachusetts, so that she might be taught to speak. Miss Fuller's method of teaching was to allow Helen to touch her (teacher's) lips, and to feel their position when she (the teacher) made a sound. Helen would then attempt to imitate her.[4]

In October 1894, Helen progressed to the Wright-Humason School for the Deaf in New York City 'for the purpose of obtaining the highest advantages in vocal culture and lip reading'. Sadly however, progress was in her words, 'not what my teachers and I had hoped and expected it would be,' and subsequently, it was only Helen's close family and friends who were able to understand her.[5]

From October 1896 until autumn 1900, Helen attended the Cambridge School for Young Ladies, after which she entered Radcliffe College, Cambridge, Massachusetts, thus becoming the first blind and deaf person ever to enrol at an institute of higher education. In June 1904, she graduated as Bachelor of Arts, having developed a keen interest in literature.

Helen also became an author, and it was at Radcliffe College that she met John Albert Macy who helped to edit her first book, *The Story of My Life*, published in 1903. In May 1905, John and Helen's friend and tutor, Anne Sullivan, were married. And when the couple set up home in Wrentham, Massachusetts, they invited Helen to join them.

Helen became a socialist and in 1913, *Out of the Dark*, her series of essays on socialism, was published. The following years would be spent on lecture tours in which she championed the cause of the poor, promoted rights for women, and railed against dangerous practices in the workplace. Her speeches were 'translated' for the public by her faithful companion Anne. To Helen, who was also a pacifist, the First World War was abhorrent. She therefore commanded the workers of the world to 'strike against manufacturing shrapnel and gas bombs and all other tools of murder. Be not dumb, obedient slaves in an army of destruction. Be heroes in an army of construction.'[6]

In 1918, Helen and the Macys moved to New York City, and Helen began a series of fundraising tours on behalf of the blind. In the same year, the office of the Permanent Blind Relief War Fund opened officially in Paris, and in 1919, its American branch was incorporated in New York State as the Permanent Blind Relief War Fund for Soldiers and Sailors of the Allies, with Helen Keller and George Kessler's wife Cora as members of its Board of Directors. The Fund gave financial support to St Dunstan's in London, and also financed schools and workshops for the blind in Belgium and France.

In 1919, Helen, presumably on the strength of what she had learnt from George and Cora Kessler, came to the UK and visited Pearson at St Dunstan's. Sidney Dark was privy to her subsequent correspondence with Pearson, and he declared that her typewriting was quite as good as that of a sighted stenographer. In one such letter, Helen told the Chief,

> You are probably tired of being told that you are the most wonderful example in the world of victory over blindness. But I should like to tell you this again. Your accomplishments will always be an incomprehensible mystery to me, though, after all, they are only the supreme proof of a point which I am never tired of making, and that is, that the greater the handicap, the greater the will and ability to surmount it, provided it is faced in the right spirit.

When Pearson sent Helen a parcel of classical novels written in Braille, she was delighted: 'I can scarcely keep my ravenous fingers off them long enough to sleep, or walk,' she declared, and compared him to the 'Three Wise Men of Versailles' (possibly a reference to characters in one of the books which Pearson had sent her). However, whereas the wise men gave away 'mere islands, cities and valleys,' Pearson, she declared, through his work for the provision of Braille books for the blind, had bestowed 'the bread of life, kingdoms of thought, and stars that shine in the darkest night! I shall only say, no one can be more grateful to another than I am to you, and shall be all my days.'

These volumes, sent by Pearson to Helen, included works by Arnold Bennett and Sir Arthur Conan Doyle. Helen's favourites, however, were those by the Russian novelists Leo Tolstoy and Ivan Turgenev. Helen was also fulsome in her praise for 'all the new work you are taking up'—i.e. other projects in addition to St Dunstan's, in which Pearson had become involved. They included

'houses of childhood' for sightless babies [and] colleges for blind girls and boys. There is something divine, universal, in the sympathy and insight with which you strive to meet every need, every aspiration of all classes of the blind.[7]

One of Helen's most memorable sayings was 'Keep your face to the sunshine and you cannot see the shadow. It's what sunflowers do.'

Richard King Huskinson

Journalist and author Richard King Huskinson, was involved with St Dunstan's almost from the time of its foundation, and his association with the organization would continue until his death in 1947. He was generally referred to as 'The Adjutant' (even though he held no official rank), or by St Dunstaners simply as 'Mr H'.

Huskinson wrote several books, including *With Silent Friends* (1917) and *Over the Fireside* (1921), both designed to draw the reader's attention to the predicament of the blind. And in what was perhaps the most important chapter of Pearson's book, *Victory Over Blindness*, he indicated just how similar his views were to those of the Chief. In respect of the blind man, he said, 'his greatest need is to be treated *normally* in his abnormal circumstances'. When depression overwhelms him, 'all that is needed is care and unobtrusive kindness—the worst will pass sooner or later; there is nothing to be done actively until it is gone'.

He continued:

> To perpetually remind him of the fact that he is blind by stupid little tactless acts and words, should be stamped out at the very first. I am convinced that more depression of spirits is caused by the so-called 'sympathy' which he gets from the outside world and his own friends than any realization of his misfortune. He depends upon the love and friendship which surround him for much of his happiness—as we all do.[1]

Death of the 'Chief'

In the final month of 1919, Pearson received a gift, which was inscribed as follows:

ON DECEMBER 15TH 1919
THE OFFICERS
NON-COMMISSIONED OFFICERS & MEN
WHO HAVE BEEN BLINDED IN THE WAR
PRESENTED TO
SIR ARTHUR PEARSON BART. G.B.E.
THIS INKSTAND
THE WRITING TABLE UPON WHICH IT STANDS,
AND THE THREE ACCOMPANYING CHAIRS,
TO FURNISH HIS OFFICE & TO REMIND HIM ALWAYS
OF THE LOVE AND GRATITUDE THEY HAVE FOR HIM
WHO LED THEM
TO
VICTORY OVER BLINDNESS

In 1920, Lady Pearson was made Dame Commander of the Order of The British Empire in recognition of her work for charity. In that year, Arsenal Football Club played a match against St Dunstan's in Regent's Park, for which members of the former team were blindfolded (apart from its goalkeeper) in order to provide a 'level playing field'. Finally, in December, Otto Kahn announced that he wished to regain possession of his property, St Dunstan's, Regent's Park.

In January 1921, St Dunstan's relocated its workshops and classrooms to St John's Lodge. By now, almost 2,000 St Dunstaners were either in training or being supported by its Aftercare Department.

In June of that year, Neville Pearson had an illegitimate daughter, Shirley Davis Spaulding by Anne Spaulding (née Davis) of New York. He would eventually marry Anne Spaulding, his third wife (by then named Anne Davis Elebash), in December 1943.[1]

Six months after the birth of his grandchild, on Friday, 9 December 1921, at the age of only fifty-five, Pearson died at his London home, 15 Devonshire Street, St Marylebone, in a tragic accident. Pearson's son Neville, stated that he had last seen his father alive at 11 p.m. the previous evening.

He was in good health and spirits. He had followed his usual occupation during the day [i.e. of visiting St Dunstan's] and had been to the theatre in the evening.

In fact, Pearson and his wife Ethel had attended a performance of Gilbert and Sullivan's opera, *The Yeoman of the Guard* at the Princes Theatre.

The circumstances of Pearson's death—as revealed at the inquest—were reported extensively in *The Times* newspaper. Pearson's final conversation was with members of his household, and it related to work he proposed to do on behalf of St Dunstan's in connection with a swimming tournament which was to take place at the nearby Marylebone Swimming Baths.[2]

Naomi Glennie, Head Parlourmaid, said that she called Sir Arthur at 7.15 [a.m. on the Friday] and took him an early cup of tea, when he seemed as usual. 'He enquired about the weather, and said which suit he would wear. He always prepared his own bath.'

Amy Campbell, his secretary, said that it was his custom to have breakfast at 8.30, but on Friday morning he did not come down, and after waiting for 10 minutes she went upstairs to see where he was. He was not in his dressing room. She saw his body in the bath, which was full of water. Consultant surgeon Sir Milsom Rees was summoned:

[He was] lying with his head under the water and face downwards. The water was discoloured with blood, and there was blood on the nozzle of the tap. There was a wound about an inch long on the right side of the forehead, which could have been caused by his falling against the tap. Death had not occurred as the direct result of the blow, but from asphyxia due to drowning.

Neville (now 'Sir') described the bath, into which the water was still running, as 'enamelled' and 'rather slippery.' In fact, only the day before his father 'had mentioned that he had previously slipped in the bath.'[3] Said Amy Campbell, 'He was a man who always liked to do things for himself. He was very independent and did not like people to help him'.

The Chief's insistence on being self-reliant and on refusing all help, if he could possibly avoid it, had probably contributed to the death of this otherwise fit and healthy man who, only the previous week had been horse-riding on the South Downs.[4] Pearson had continued to work for the blind right up until the end; his final public duty having been to open Hoole Bank Home for the Blind at Chester in Cheshire in the North of England.

At a Committee Meeting, held on the very day of Pearson's death, Colonel Ball proposed that Lord Chaplin take the Chair, whereupon His Lordship declared,

We have lost at the head of this Association, which has done such infinite good, one of the best men that ever lived, and one whose skill in conducting it could never have been surpassed by anyone that we have ever known.[5]

At a special meeting of the Committee, convened on 12 December 1921, Lord Chaplin proposed that Sir Neville Pearson should take the Chair. The following resolutions were put forward: That Lady Pearson DBE be appointed President of St Dunstan's Hostel for Blinded Soldiers & Sailors;[6] Sir Neville Pearson be appointed a Vice-President and Honorary Treasurer of the Blinded Soldiers & Sailors Care Committee;[7] Sir Washington Ranger (who had received a knighthood in 1918) be appointed a Vice-President; and twenty-four-year-old Captain Ian Fraser be appointed Chairman.[8] However, Washington Ranger's son, Sir Vincent Ranger, told the Committee that his father considered that the post of Vice-President would impose 'too great a tax upon his strength, and he would prefer to occupy a more or less honorary position'.

As regards the launch of an Appeal for the establishment of an Endowment Fund in memory of his late father, Sir Neville stated that both he and Lady Pearson felt strongly that such a memorial

> should take the form of a vigorous effort to put Sir Arthur's work on an assured basis. The present suggestion was, that the Appeal should be world-wide.... At present the suggestion is that the monies collected should be divided as to one-third to St Dunstans, one-third to the National Institute for the Blind, and one-third for all other blind Charities in the Empire. [However] prior to these divisions it is suggested that two and a half per cent should be deducted for the benefit of the Fresh Air Fund which was my father's first Charity.[9]

The 'Sir Arthur Pearson Memorial Fund' was launched in 1923.

Messages of condolence were received from King George V and Queen Mary, Prime Minister David Lloyd George, the Mayor of St Marylebone, the Associations of South African Blinded Soldiers, New Zealand Blinded Soldiers, Australian Red Cross, Institution for Belgian War Blinded, American Permanent Blind Relief War Fund, High Commissioners of the British Dominions, innumerable institutions for the blind scattered throughout the British Empire, and from those concerned with the welfare of the blind in all parts of the world. However, as Sidney Dark pointed out, 'deep as was the sorrow for the death of Arthur Pearson among his fellow-citizens who could see, deeper still was it among his comrades who were blind'.

The funeral service was held at the local church, Holy Trinity in Marylebone Road. The mourners included Lady Pearson, the three daughters of her previous marriage (Isla, Muriel, and Nora), and Sir Neville, together with nearly 1,200 blinded St Dunstaners, past and present. (The latter were accommodated in a large dormitory specially erected for the purpose in the grounds of St Dunstan's, and 200 men of the Guards Brigade volunteered to act as guides for them during their stay in London.) Queen Alexandra, St Dunstan's patron, sent a wreath.

Before the flower-covered coffin, as it was borne up the aisle, walked a Boy Scout with a wreath in the form of a Union Jack, the staff of which supported a dove carrying the emblematic device 'V.O.B.' which stood for 'Victory Over Blindness'—Sir Arthur's favourite motto, and also that of St Dunstan's.[10]

The service was conducted by the Bishop of London, The Reverend Prebendary E. N. Sharpe, together with The Reverend Harold Gibb, a former St Dunstaner. Gibb had been blinded on 15 May 1915 in the Battle of Potijze (2nd Battle of Ypres) while serving as chaplain/

Pearson's funeral: Ian Fraser escorted by a Scout. (*Blind Veterans UK*)

Pearson's funeral. (*Blind Veterans UK*)

combatant officer to the 4th Royal Irish Dragoon Guards. However, it was not until September 1917 that he was admitted to St Dunstan's. The reason for the delay was that he was required to stand in for his vicar who had taken up an appointment with the YMCA.

Their Majesties King George V and Queen Mary, Queen Alexandra, the Queen of Norway, and the Prince of Wales all sent representatives. George Ridding, Pearson's former headmaster from Winchester College and then Bishop of Southwell, was present, as were Sir Robert Baden-Powell, founder of the Boy Scout Movement, several cabinet ministers, and several high commissioners from the dominions.

Pearson was buried at Hampstead Cemetery. At his graveside The Reverend J. A. Williams, Chaplain to St Dunstan's, said a prayer. After this, led by the band of the 1st Battalion Grenadier Guards, the Reverend John Henry Newman's hymn 'Lead Kindly Light', was sung.

> Lead, kindly Light, amid the encircling gloom,
>> Lead Thou me on;
> The night is dark, and I am far from home,
>> Lead Thou me on.
> Keep Thou my feet; I do not ask to see
>> The distant scene; one step enough for me.

If ever there was a hymn appropriate for an occasion, this was it.

From the press and public alike, praise for Pearson was unstinting. In *The Times* obituary was written,

> He was an exceedingly active man, a fine horseman, a swimmer, and a player of the most exercising games he could find. All that he learned from his own suffering, he lavished on his fellow sufferers; and he made his private loss the world's gain. His maxim was, 'Blindness is an opportunity.' He made St Dunstan's a household word. Newspaper proprietors gladly helped their former colleague, giving him the publicity that he needed. During the war one could hardly pick up a newspaper without finding a reference in it to St Dunstan's and its work.
>
> Declaring that Pearson would have none of the existing practice—he said it existed—of treating them [the blind] as a God-afflicted class, whose needs were confined to religious instruction. He said ... that he had received more from St Dunstan's than he had given.[11]

The *Daily Mail* stated that Pearson would be remembered chiefly

> for his quiet sacrifice of all ease and leisure and his own desire to help and comfort, not only the stricken soldiers, but the blind all the world over. Few men have won gratitude more enduring; none is more grievously mourned today.

The *Daily Herald* said of Pearson,

> his triumph over darkness and the wonderful way in which he carried on with the normal detail of life were the fruits of an admirable and indomitable courage.

Ernest Kessell, Treasurer of St Dunstan's, was quoted in the *Daily Graphic*, in an article by Hannen Swaffer:

> If he [Pearson] had not been blind, he could never have brought the power and happiness into other men's lives as he did. He made his own misfortune a blessing for others, because, like the men who came to him, he himself had once seen and now was sightless.

Sir Washington Ranger referred to Pearson's willpower, and to the 'watchful care' which he took in matters relating to his work. It was, he said, 'the subject of amazement and admiration on the part of all who were privileged to be his colleagues [and to his] brilliant brain and great heart'.

Ralph Blumenfeld, writing in the *Daily Express*, described Pearson as 'a man of achievement, strong, vivid, a radiant figure of energy, enthusiasm and human affection … one of those rare men who are born for a purpose'.[12]

Sir Robert Baden-Powell acknowledged that it was Pearson who had encouraged him to found the Boy Scout Movement.[13] Pearson's obituary was published on 13 February 1922 in *The Wykehamist*, the magazine of his former school, Winchester College:

> Of all Wykehamists of recent years, there is no one who has been more conspicuous in the popular eye than Cyril Arthur Pearson; there are few of whom Winchester has more reason to be proud.

And in regard to his time at St Dunstan's:

> He was himself the soul of the whole company; and he made a point of knowing closely all the 1,400 men who were trained there. A quarter of an hour with Pearson changed their whole outlook on life. 'He gave us,' says one of the St Dunstaners, 'light for darkness, courage for despair'.[14]

Finally, South African St Dunstaner Hugh Stayt paid this moving tribute to the Chief:

To Sir Arthur Pearson

The darken'd clouds of war rolled by,
And hid our earth from God's bright sky,
Whilst on the field of battle silent stood
Our Nation's flower, both strong and good.

Then hell was loos'd and brave men died,
The laws of God were all defiled.
And limb and sight were sacrificed,
Because we fought for right and Christ.

And then back home, there streamed the blind,
And we thought God had been unkind.
But to our dying hopes there came
A man who had been served the same.

He made us feel that we were still
Brave men, and like him, had a will.
And like a ray of heavenly light,
He taught us how to lose our sight.

And now his work has been well done,
Great fame and honour he has won.
And tho' he's gone, our precious ray,
We know again we'll meet some day.

Throughout the world, he's proved his worth,
By helping us upon this earth.
And we shall ne'er forget that name,
Who gave St Dunstan's life and fame.[15]

Pearson's tombstone consists of a tall stone cross, mounted on a tiered stone plinth. It bears the simple inscription:

For ever blessed
SIR CYRIL ARTHUR PEARSON
FIRST BARONET OF ST DUNSTAN'S C.B.E.

On the vertical arm of the cross is depicted a flaming torch—the emblem of St Dunstan's.

St Dunstan's Without Pearson

Now that Pearson was no more, what would be the fate of St Dunstan's? Could the organization survive the death of the Chief? The answer was yes, and for several reasons. Pearson had projected St Dunstan's into the minds of the public, and it had captured their imagination. He had also altered the public perception of a blind man—formerly as one only fit to sell matches on street corners—by proving that the blind could develop skills which are of value to the community and play a full part in that community.

Therefore, with the goodwill and support of the people and the endorsement of notable figures of the day, not least of the Royal family, St Dunstan's would continue, despite the tragic loss of its founder and leading light. And it was vital that it should, as the requirements of St Dunstaners were ongoing.

Although he could not have foreseen his untimely death, Pearson had shown foresight in recognizing Ian Fraser's talent and appointing him (unofficially) as his heir apparent. Here was someone who would make sure that St Dunstan's was kept 'high profile' in the public eye. As for the future, as MP for St Pancras North (1922–29, 1931–36), Fraser was to represent and fight for the organization at the highest level. But the road ahead would not be easy. For example, the commencement of Fraser's chairmanship coincided with a national economic slump, and also with a downturn in St Dunstan's finances. In his words, 'war charities are naturally among the major casualties of peace'.[1] Economies had therefore to be made, and the outcome was that the annexes at Cheltenham, North Berwick, and Ilkley were closed, with the consequent loss of accommodation for about 150 men. However, on the positive side, an employment bureau was created in order to help men trained as telephonists and stenographers find suitable posts. A massage and electrotherapeutic clinic was established at 18 Christopher Street in Finsbury Square, employing one sighted masseur and a number of blind ones.

Some 200 St Dunstaners became poultry farmers: at first at Dollis Hill, London, and later at Kings Langley in Hertfordshire; six per cent were trained as homecraft workers; a hundred and thirty trained as masseurs and were initially employed in military hospitals, but they subsequently faced problems as these institutions became redundant and closed down. During the 1940s, physiotherapy training at St Dunstan's was supplemented by an additional two years of training at London's Royal National Institute for the Blind's School of Physiotherapy.

Much of St Dunstan's income was spent on establishing and equipping workshops for its trained men in their own home areas; this was seen as preferable to letting them try—and fail—to find their own places of work, and thus to fall into unemployment.[2]

In 1922, when ophthalmologist Sir Arnold Lawson, in accordance with the Chief's wishes, published his book *War Blindness at St Dunstan's*, he paid this tribute to the Chief:

> I offer this result of my endeavour to the illustrious memory of the Great Founder of St Dunstan's, a man whose life was given to others, that they, like he, should see light in darkness.

In June 1922, St Dunstan's was incorporated as a company, and its powers extended to enable it to give assistance to 'sailors, airmen, and other persons blinded in or as a consequence of the Great War of 1914–1918 or in any other war or war-like operations'. In Canada, St Dunstaner Walter C. ('Bill') Dies founded the Sir Arthur Pearson Club of Blinded Soldiers and Sailors (of which he became president on no less than four separate occasions) with its headquarters at the CNIB's National Office, Beverley Street, Toronto, by mutual consent.

Also in that year, Sir Neville married the Honourable Mary Angela Mond (1901–37), daughter of Minister of Health Sir Alfred Moritz Mond, 1st Baron Melchett, and his wife Violet. Mary bore him two children: Anne (born 1923), and Nigel Arthur (born 1925).[3]

In 1923, Agnes Mary Peters was accepted for training at Brighton. She thus became, as far as is known, the first female St Dunstaner. It had been agreed that women who suffered from loss of sight as a result of working in munitions factories should qualify for admission, and Agnes had been blinded and severely burnt in an explosion at Woolwich Arsenal ordnance factory in London, in February 1917.

In 1923, the Duke of York (later to become King George VI) visited St Dunstan's for the first time, and two years later St Dunstaners received the sad news that Queen Alexandra had died. St Dunstan's would now have no patron until the year 1936.

Agnes Mary Peters. (*Blind Veterans UK*)

St Dunstan's 1923: The Duke of York (third from left) witnessing a rope-climbing competition. (*Blind Veterans UK*)

Sir Ian Fraser and Sir Neville Pearson. (*Blind Veterans UK*)

In early 1927, Lady Pearson achieved what her late husband had longed to do—pay a visit to the antipodes; in company with the Duke and Duchess of York, she travelled to New Zealand. On 18 February they visited the Jubilee Institute for the Blind in Auckland.

In that year, West House was enlarged to accommodate ninety men and Sir Neville (now divorced) fulfilled his boyhood dream and married actress Gladys Buckmaster (née Cooper)—she being likewise divorced. She bore him a daughter, Sally. Sadly, the marriage would only last until 1936. In 1932, Sir Neville became Honorary Treasurer of St Dunstan's.

In 1929 the Australian Blinded Soldiers Association, which had been founded eight years previously, was inaugurated. Its authority was 'vested in a Council comprising of two councillors from each State body, a President, a Vice-President, and a Secretary/Treasurer'.[4] The ABSA held a biennial national conference, each State taking its turn to play host.

In 1930, William G. Askew was appointed Secretary of St Dunstan's and the office of General Manager merged with his own. 'There is no single individual member of the staff to whom St Dunstan's owes more than Mr Askew,' said Fraser.[5] In that year, St Dunstan's Regent's Park was purchased by Lord Rothermere and Ellen Chadwick Bates, Secretary of St Dunstan's, relocated to South Africa where she succeeded Charles Vintcent as Secretary of the St Dunstan's Aftercare Committee.

In the 1930s the numerous activities in which St Dunstaners were invited to participate included: the annual sports day in Regent's Park; the Armistice dances; swimming galas; visits to the annual 'Varsity' rugby football match between Oxford and Cambridge; holiday camping under canvas; reunions and reunion dinners for the shorthand typists, masseurs, and telephonists; the FA Cup Final; country walks; darts; debating clubs; annual regatta and inter-club competitions; 'coach rambles', and musical concerts. In addition, Arsenal FC was in the habit of generously donating tickets for a number of matches throughout the season.

In January 1931, Fraser, together with Clutha Mackenzie, travelled to the USA to lay a wreath at the Tomb of the Unknown Soldier at Arlington, Virginia. In that year, Fraser was again elected MP (until 1937) for North St Pancras.

In 1931 St Dunstan's Aftercare Committee in George, Western Cape, was dissolved, and a new committee was formed in Cape Town. The need for facilities such as this was still critical: during 1932 there were nineteen new admissions, including five 'mustard gas cases', the pernicious effects of which had been delayed for fifteen years or more.

It had been customary for St Dunstan's to present each St Dunstaner with a crystal set and headphones, but in 1933 the Council agreed to replace these listening devices with a wireless set and loudspeaker.

In 1934, 2,000 or so ex-servicemen and women were under the care of St Dunstan's. Ian Fraser received a knighthood having successfully introduced the Blind Voter Bill, whereby a blind person was permitted to vote in a polling booth, provided that he or she was in the presence of a relative or friend. Meanwhile, St Dunstan's, together with the NIB, produced its first 'talking book'—in the form of a gramophone record. Subsequently, and with the generous help of motor car magnate and philanthropist Lord Nuffield, a library of such items for the use of the blind was created. In fact, Lord Nuffield donated an annual sum of £5,000 for seven years to the Talking Book Library, and in later years, His Lordship helped fund the transition from gramophone to tape recordings.

Ian Fraser, CBE, and Clutha MacKenzie visiting the Tomb of the Unknown Soldier at Arlington National Cemetery, Washington DC, 1931. (*Royal New Zealand Foundation of the Blind*)

In November the 'Empire Blinded Soldiers' Conference', organized by the ABSA, was held in Melbourne, with the Duke of Gloucester, Sir Ian Fraser, and Sir Clutha Mackenzie and forty or so war-blinded ex-servicemen in attendance. In that same year, the hostel for blinded servicemen in Auckland's Titoki Street was renamed 'Pearson House'.

With the prospect looming of another war with Germany, plans were put in place for a new, state-of-the-art, six-storey, 130-bed facility to be constructed on a 12-acre site on the outskirts of Brighton. St Dunstan's, Ovingdean, complete with modern workshops, recreation rooms, and swimming pool, would serve as a holiday and convalescent home, and also a training centre. No expense was spared, for example, to provide guide rails, rubber-edged doors and safety gates on its stairways.[6]

In 1935, St Dunstan's established a programme for training St Dunstaners in the use of routers, vertical belt sanders, and circular saws.[7] The skills thereby acquired by the men would serve the country well in the forthcoming dark days of war. In that year, Lord Rothermere decided to return St Dunstan's clock to its original owner, the Church of St Dunstan-in-the-West.[8]

On 20 January 1936, King George V died and was succeeded by his son, King Edward VIII. Edward, hitherto a stalwart supporter of St Dunstan's, now became its patron. The patronage was short-lived, however, and upon Edward's abdication on 10 December 1936, his brother, the new King George VI, became Patron of St Dunstan's.

Meanwhile, St Dunstan's, Regent's Park (the organization premises in the early days) was destroyed in a fire. It was replaced by Winfield House—Woolworth heiress Barbara Hutton having purchased the site on which to build a home for herself.

From 11–13 May 1937 a reunion was held in Christchurch for the blinded soldiers of New Zealand, 'arranged by the Trustees of the Commercial Travellers' and Warehousemen's

Blinded Soldiers' Fund, in association with the New Zealand Institute for the Blind'. Sir Ian Fraser was thanked for his 'cordial greetings and good wishes', sent on behalf of St Dunstan's,[9] and the following report was made:

> The St Dunstan's group in New Zealand numbers twenty-eight, of whom eighteen had their happy months of training at St Dunstan's, and ten, losing their sight after their return to the Dominion, are newer, but just as enthusiastic, members.[10]

On 27 June 1937 two hundred St Dunstaners 'took part in the Review of eighty thousand ex-Service men by His Majesty the King in Hyde Park. One hundred men came from London, and the remainder from other parts of the country. All were chosen by ballot.'[11] Another parade of this kind took place on 5 July 1937 in Edinburgh, and was also attended by St Dunstaners:

> Led by Captain William Appleby, member of the Executive Council of St Dunstan's, thirty Scottish St Dunstaners took part in the parade of Regular troops and ex-Service men when the King made his State journey from Edinburgh to Holyrood House. [Having marched] to the Palace, where a special position in the forecourt had been allotted to them, there, with war-blinded men from Newington House, and the Guard of Honour of the 1st Battalion Gordon Highlanders, they awaited the arrival of Their Majesties [King George VI and Queen Elizabeth].[12]

In 1936, Fraser visited Berlin on the invitation of the German War Victims Care Association. In July 1937, the invitation was reciprocated in an event of great significance, as described by Fraser:

> During the past fortnight we have welcomed to Headquarters [St John's Lodge, Regent's Park] a party of German ex-Servicemen — two of them blinded in the War. They were Herr August Martens, leader of the German War-Blind Organization, Herr Hans F. W. Voigt, District Leader of the Hamburg and surrounding districts Organization, and Herr Von Cossell, Chief Adjutant to Herr Oberlindober, the Leader of the German Ex-Servicemen's Organization. Herr Martens and Herr Voigt were blinded during the War. Herr Voigt was accompanied by his wife, Frau Voigt, and his son, Dr Heinz Voigt, who acted as interpreter.
>   We were taking our small part in carrying out the wishes expressed by the King that contacts between ex-service men of all countries should be made.
>   The party arrived in London early on Tuesday morning, July 13th, and after they had been welcomed at their hotel by Sir Neville Pearson, Colonel Eric Ball, Sir Ian and Lady Fraser, and Mr Askew, they came on to Headquarters where they made an extensive tour of the building.

That evening, the visiting party of Germans attended a 'Rowing Dinner'—i.e. for the oarsmen of St Dunstan's.

> During the three or four days the Germans are in London they have visited [St Dunstan's] Headquarters and Raglan Street [where new premises for workshops and stores had been

obtained], and the National Institute for the Blind to obtain all the information they can. The German Leaders said, 'We have learned much that will be of great value to us for the Aftercare of our blinded men'.

On Friday morning the visitors went to the Cenotaph in Whitehall where they placed a wreath.

The visitors also attended the Annual Regatta at Putney, as did Lady Pearson:

> Sir Ian Fraser gave a welcome to everyone present, and then called upon Colonel Eric Ball, senior member of St Dunstan's Council. Speaking in German, Colonel Ball gave a hearty welcome to our German friends, and referred to His Majesty's expressed wish that old soldiers would continue to make contacts all over the world to promote peace. 'We meet now,' he said, 'in the most friendly manner to try and understand each other better, and promote good relations between our two countries. We hope also that the things you have been shown at St Dunstan's will contribute something towards the wellbeing of German blinded soldiers and other blind persons in Germany. We in our turn have gained much from our contacts with you.'
>
> Herr Hans F. W. Voigt... also spoke of his pleasure at meeting St Dunstan's' men.[13]

If there was ever a testament to the futility of war, this was it. And how ironic, bearing in mind that in two years' time, the two countries would once again be at war with each other.

An invitation to the war-blinded men of Britain to visit their war-blinded counterparts in Germany was 'cordially accepted', and on Saturday 23 July 1937, St Dunstaners Wilfred Nash of Hastings, Albert C. Evans of Newport, Monmouthshire, and Duncan Maclean of Brimpton, near Reading, set off from St Dunstan's for the Continent. On their return, MacLean declared,

> What we did discover was that there is no doubt as to the sincerity of the German people to be friends with England, and they are no less sincere in their desire for true peace, but you must go to Germany to prove that.

Said Evans,

> During our visit to the German Blinded Soldiers' Homes we had an opportunity of meeting a few of the 3,500 who were blinded through war service. We only visited two of the five Homes used by the German comrades. The first we visited was at Berlin and is known as the Headquarters. It is a lovely house situated not far from the centre of Berlin, standing in its own grounds. This house was presented to the blinded soldiers by Herr Hitler, who himself was blind for two months during the war from gas. This home takes his name.[14]

On Monday 6 September 1937, Lady Pearson laid the foundation stone of what would become St Dunstan's, Ovingdean, Brighton. In August 1938 the men vacated West House, and in the second week of October, they transferred to the newly opened St Dunstan's, Ovingdean. West House would now become the St Dunstan's Aftercare Department.

The Second World War

The First World War was described as 'the war to end all wars', but now the nightmare was to begin again. However, the outbreak of the Second World War in September 1939 found St Dunstan's well prepared. By the generosity of Lord Nuffield, a new hospital wing, complete with an up-to-date operating theatre, was added to St Dunstan's, Ovingdean. Said Fraser,

> All soldiers, sailors and airmen of all the Home and Dominion Forces who may be blinded in this war will go to St Dunstan's Hospital for surgical and medical treatment, and to learn to be blind [i.e. how to live with their blindness] during their early days. But as soon as they are fit enough for serious training, the Scotsmen who intend to live in Scotland will go to Newington House for training, and those from England and Wales and the Dominions will pass from the Hospital side of St Dunstan's into the Training Establishment.[1]

During the period of hostilities it was decided that certain civilians should also be eligible for membership of St Dunstan's. Included were those working for the following services: fire, police, nursing, Air Raid Precaution (ARP), Home Guard, ambulance, first aid, rescue, Royal Observer Corps, Civil Nursing Reserve.[2] Also, civilians who had suffered loss of sight as a result of eye injuries sustained in air raids, or as a result of accidents occurring in munitions factories—where explosions were not uncommon.

India had for a long time been a part of the Empire largely overlooked in terms of support services for blinded soldiers. Fraser explains how this changed with the start of the Second World War:

> Sir Clutha Mackenzie happened to be on holiday in India in September 1939. I invited him to stay five or six months to take charge of our new appeal, and he stayed the whole War; but not just raising funds. He created, almost single-handed, a St Dunstan's for blinded Indian servicemen. The Indian Army responded by placing at Mackenzie's disposal a former P.O.W. camp at Dehra Dun, 120 miles north of Delhi in the foothills of the Himalayas.

Meanwhile, from 1940–42, Mackenzie undertook a lecture tour of the USA, raising funds for St Dunstan's. In late 1942, Mackenzie was asked by the Indian Government 'to carry out a review of the Indian blind world as a whole, and draw up plans for the post-war welfare of the Indian civilian blind'.

In June 1943, St Dunstan's' Training Centre for War Blinded, Dehra Dun, was duly opened, its first admission being Havildar Abdul Karim. Over the next two years, another seventy blinded Indian servicemen would follow, together with an Englishman who was transferred to Church Stretton (see below). The men 'came from all over the sub-continent, were of different races and religions, and represented six separate language groups'.

At Dehra Dun, the men were taught to read, write, and typewrite in Urdu, this being a language used throughout India, whatever a person's native tongue might be. Music lessons were provided, and 'they had their first concert a few months after opening, and the success of it was Clutha Mackenzie's first reward.'

Four Maharattas (116th Maharattas, an infantry regiment of the British Indian Army) were among the first men to complete their training, and they duly travelled home to Southern Bombay, each 'equipped with a piano-accordion, a braille watch, a small loom for the weaving of newar—a webbing which takes the place of wire springs in Indian beds—and a supply of cotton yarn'.

Early in 1945 came a surprise in the form of Lance-Naik Karam Singh. He had been blinded at Gallipoli in 1915, and been awarded the Indian Order of Merit for his gallantry. 'He had heard of St Dunstan's [Dehra Dun] and wrote to know if he might come. Aged sixty, he is quite undefeated, and he set himself a programme of weaving, music, and braille.'[3]

In the early 1950s, Mackenzie was employed by UNESCO in Paris, where he worked to create a universal system of Braille notation. From 1952 to 1964, he chaired the World Braille Council.

Meanwhile the *St Dunstan's Review* of February 1940 contained the names of the sons of St Dunstaners who were currently serving in the armed services. There were forty-six in all, and often more than one from the same family. The list would grow longer as the war dragged on, and soon, many of them would be numbered among those killed in action.[4]

In April 1940 it was reported that Sir Neville Pearson, who had 'rejoined his old arm of the Service before the present war broke out', was now serving in the Anti-Aircraft Artillery and had been promoted to the rank of major.[5] St Dunstaners helped in whichever ways they could, and in May 1940 no less than 116 St Dunstaners were engaged in producing fifty camouflage nets per week for the war effort.[6]

Brighton, situated as it is on the south coast, was in danger of enemy attack from both air and sea, and in mid-1940 it was decided that precautionary steps needed to be taken. Fraser described what these steps were to be:

The building at Ovingdean, Brighton, will remain St Dunstan's Hospital for serious eye or head injuries requiring operative treatment arising out of the present war, or for old St Dunstaners suffering from similar conditions.

The training of blinded soldiers has been moved to a moderate-sized Hotel, which we have taken, called The Longmynd Hotel, Church Stretton, Shropshire. Great War St Dunstaners who have only recently gone blind, and the convalescent casualties from the new war, have been moved there. These include some who have been totally blinded in the recent fighting, some who have been temporarily or partially blinded, and others who are recovering.

The bed-ridden and similar cases who lived permanently at Ovingdean have been transferred to a small, quiet country house, called Melplash Court, Nr. Beaminster, Dorset.

Lady St Dunstaners at Church Stretton, left to right: Gwen Obern, Vi Delaney, Barbara Bell, Brenda Rea, Thelma Meredith, and Elsie Aldred.

A small Hotel has been taken in Blackpool, called the Concord Hotel, 1 Wimbourne Crescent, South Shore, Blackpool, for a convalescent home. An office has been opened at Blackpool, from which the whole of the Aftercare Services for St Dunstaners who live in the Midlands and the North will be conducted.

The Brighton Office [West House], at Portland Place, Kemp Town, Brighton, will remain open, and Mr Askew [Secretary of St Dunstan's] will attend to all official and general matters from there. Mr H. M. Day and Mrs Paul will remain at Brighton in charge of all welfare matters for those in the South.

The Massage, Poultry Farm, and Estate Offices will all remain at Brighton.

The Chairman's Office and the Appeals Office remain in London, at Regent's Park, and I shall continue to work from there. Raglan Street will continue to function as usual.[7]

At Church Stretton, operations expanded when St Dunstan's acquired Tiger Hall, a substantial property which was transformed into a hospital, and several other buildings in the town. Meanwhile, rowing activities resumed; this time on the River Severn for one afternoon per week, with pupils from Shrewsbury School acting as coxwains.

In summer 1940, in a debate in Parliament on the subject of war pensions,

Sir Ian Fraser made an important speech in which he demanded that the pensions of new[ly] blinded soldiers, sailors and airmen must be 'brought up to the level of those of the Great War men'.[8]

On the night of 10 September 1940, a bomb fell just outside the gate of St Dunstan's headquarters at St John's Lodge, Regent's Park, leaving a huge crater and causing superficial damage to the building.[9] There is a saying, 'lightning does not strike twice in the same place,' but the following month, said Fraser,

> a bomb fell directly on the Talking Book recording rooms, which are part of our main buildings. The studios, recording rooms, experimental workshop, proof-reading room, were all completely destroyed. Of course, we intend to carry on. This is the spirit of Britain and the spirit of St Dunstan's. We are immediately setting to work to start again, but it will be a month or two before we can get into production. This direct hit has badly damaged the whole of our building and my house—St Dunstaners will remember that my own private house is next door to the Headquarters building [Fraser and his wife having previously occupied the middle floor of St John' Lodge]—and we have temporarily moved the greater part of the office to the old St John's Lodge building, which had been turned into a museum and happened to be empty.[10]

Four months earlier, on 29 May 1940, St Dunstan's had admitted its first Polish soldier, Jan Lasowski of the Chasseurs de Montagne, who had been wounded at Narvik, Norway, and totally blinded. In December he was 'decorated by General Sikorski [Prime Minister of the Polish Government in Exile and Commander-in-Chief of the Polish Armed Forces] with the equivalent to the British VC for his conspicuous bravery at Narvik'.[11]

In June 1940, Fraser was elected Member of Parliament for Lonsdale (and from 1950–58 he served as MP for Morecambe and Lonsdale). 'There was one group of men that we could not reach,' he said, 'and they caused me more concern than any others'. He was referring to war-blinded prisoners of war. He was adamant that attempts had to be made to discover their names and whereabouts, and to offer them assistance: 'It was urgently necessary for us to do all we could to break the monotony and probable despondency of these men.' In order to do this it would be necessary to enlist the help of the Red Cross.[12] But further assistance would also come from a most unlikely source.

Oswald Phipps, 4th Marquis of Normanby, was an officer in the Green Howards. On 5 June 1940, during the retreat to Dunkirk, he sustained a serious wound to his leg and was subsequently captured.

Normanby was admitted to Reserve-Lazaret IX-C, a hospital at Obermassfeld, Thuringia, in central Germany (administered by Stalag IX-C, a prisoner of war camp for Allied prisoners). The hospital was administered by British, Canadian, and New Zealand medical staff. At the camp, Normanby discovered that three of his fellow POWs had been blinded, and he took it upon himself to teach them Braille with the use of a Braille alphabet (which he discovered in a Larousse French language encyclopaedic dictionary in the camp library), some cardboard, and some matchsticks. The three men were Jimmy Shepherd, Douglas Parmenter, and Frederick Wareham.

Although Normanby was fluent in German, he refused to speak the language and insisted on using an interpreter. Nonetheless, he was able to persuade the German authorities to send all war-blinded Allied POWs (there were eventually twenty-eight all told) to Obermassfeld. Furthermore, he was permitted to liaise with Fraser in respect of the men's needs.[13] In 1942, the patients at Obermassfeld Hospital were relocated to Kloster Haina, near Kassel, Hesse (administered by Stalag IX-A), in central Germany.

Lord Normanby (back row, left), Obermassfeld Hospital, Germany, with other blinded Allied POWs. (*The Marquis of Normanby*)

Lieutenant-Colonel Michael P. Ansell, commander of the 1st Lothian and Border Yeomanry and, at thirty-five, the youngest commander in the British Army, was covering the retreat to Dunkirk (27 May–4 June 1940) when he and some comrades hid in the loft of a French farmhouse to avoid capture by the advancing German forces. Unfortunately, the local people mistook them for the enemy, and tipped off some other British would-be escapers who fired up into the loft space. Ansell was partially blinded and wounded in both hands by this so-called 'friendly fire'. He therefore had no choice but to surrender to the enemy.

Ansell became a POW in various hospitals and in Oflag 9A POW camp at Schloss Spangenburg near Kassel, Hesse. He was later imprisoned at Stalag 8B, Lamsdorf POW camp, in Poland, where he came under the care of ophthalmic surgeon Major David Charters of the Royal Army Medical Corps, a fellow POW who had been captured in Greece in 1941. It was Charters, said Ansell, who attempted unsuccessfully 'to remove the clots of blood from my eyes'. Ansell was now returned to Oflag 9A. Subsequently, he was transferred to the Templehof military hospital, Berlin, where he was examined by 'one of the greatest German eye specialists [unidentified]'.[14]

Finally, Ansell was transferred to Kloster Haina, where he again (together with the camp's other blind POWs) came under the care of Major Charters who had himself been transferred there, and where he met Lord Normanby, who he described as 'the force' behind the care of the blinded POWs.[15]

At Kloster Haina, the Germans co-operated by providing one of their own officers (who had himself been partially blinded) to assist with the teaching of Braille—including shorthand— and typewriting, permitting the blinded men to take walks outdoors, and allowing them to form a band, with the aid of musical instruments provided by the Red Cross (which was the only organization permitted by the Germans to have contact with enemy prison camps). The men were also provided with books printed in Braille (and could even choose to learn the subject by correspondence course), specially made dominoes and playing cards, and eye-shades and eye drops for those recovering from blindness.[16] Also, the men formed a debating society and 'put on plays to entertain the rest of the camp'.[17] As for Ansell, with seeds supplied by the Royal Horticultural Society, and with tools supplied by Mme Tiberghine, a friend of the French Resistance in Paris (both via the Red Cross), he created a flower garden at the camp.[18]

The blinded servicemen in Italian POW camps were less well equipped. Fraser said, 'we were not able to do much for them, but the Red Cross took them Braille watches and reading matter, typewriters and games'.[19]

On 19 July 1940, with the approval of the Charity Commissioners, St Dunstan's was permitted to extend its reach and assist 'other persons including women and other non-combatants blinded in or as a consequence of the Great War of 1914–1918 or in any other war or warlike operations'.

The South Africa National Council for the Blind, under the continuing chairmanship of First World War St Dunstaner Robert ('Mike') Bowen, expanded its activities to meet the needs of the returning South African war blinded.

Meanwhile, early in 1941 it was decided that any war-blinded casualties arriving in South Africa were to be admitted to the military hospital at Wynberg, Cape Town, prior to their transportation by hospital ship back to Britain. It now fell to Ellen Chadwick Bates to establish a training centre for them there. Furthermore, building contractor Norman Kennedy of Wynberg loaned his mansion 'Tembani'—meaning, in the Xhosa language, 'To hope and to go on hoping'—complete with 3 acres of gardens, to St Dunstan's for the duration of the war. With accommodation for eight residents, it was formally opened on 18 February 1942. Subsequently, huts were erected in the grounds to serve as classrooms and workshops.[20]

In March 1941, William V. C. Ruxton, President of the British American Ambulance Corps, 'through his London representative, Mrs Somerville Smith, presented an Ambulance to St Dunstan's Hospital. This beautifully-equipped and efficient vehicle was delivered at Church Stretton on Monday, March 24th.' This was not the only support Mr Ruxton gave:

St Dunstaners will remember that Mr and Mrs Ruxton are the owners of [the aforementioned] Melplash Court, Bridport, which they have lent to us for the duration of the war as a West Country Convalescent Home.[21]

In April 1941, Fraser paid tribute to 'the abundant generosity of the American people'. For example, Mr Robert R. Appleby, Chairman of the British War Relief Society in New York, and Mrs Rex Benson and Mr Bertram de N. Cruger, the Society's representatives in London, had taken a 'sympathetic interest in our work'. As a result, said Fraser, 'The British War Relief Society has made us a grant of £25,000'.[22]

In May 1941, Fraser reported that St Dunstan's had requested both the Red Cross and the Order of St John War Organization to conduct an agreed scheme of help to the British blinded prisoners of war now in Germany, through their Invalid Comforts Section,[23] which has special facilities, and it is hoped shortly to get this functioning.

The scheme includes the provision of invalid comforts, gifts of braille watches, special ridged paper to enable the prisoner to write home, and the teaching of braille reading through correspondence with the aid of sighted prisoners of war who will be asked to act as teachers.[24]

In addition, Fraser sent each blinded POW a letter explaining what St Dunstan's could offer him on his release and repatriation to Britain, together with a St Dunstan's badge—with its motif of a flaming torch.[25] In this way, in the heart of enemy territory, the light of the torch of St Dunstan's burned brightly.

On 19 August 1941 actor Esmond Knight was admitted to Church Stretton. As a lieutenant in the Royal Naval Volunteer Reserve, he had been wounded and blinded the previous May during the battle of the Denmark Strait, which had culminated in the sinking of the German battleship *Bismarck*. Knight was taught Braille and typewriting, and in his spare time he contributed enthusiastically to the St Dunstan's amateur dramatic society. Although he was completely blind for two years, Knight subsequently regained a degree of sight in his right eye, and when the war ended he made a successful return to stage and screen.

In that year the Princess Royal visited St Dunstan's. Also in that year, Sir Neville's daughter Shirley was married to Rutherford Hatch (1892–74) of New York—a member of the wealthy Vanderbilt family. Shirley's second marriage was to New York Lawyer Wyndham Lewis Gary (died 1989). In the 1940s, Shirley was editor of *Fashion Trades*, the New York fashion industry newspaper. In her later years, as contributing editor for the *Braille Mirror* (a publication of the Braille Institute for which she served on its Board of Directors), she carried on the Pearson family tradition of performing good works on behalf of the blind.[26]

In 1942 in Canada, the Sir Arthur Pearson Club of Blinded Soldiers and Sailors was renamed the Sir Arthur Pearson Association of War Blinded, so that veterans of the present war might be included.

In November 1942, two huts were constructed at Church Stretton so that St Dunstaners could be taught manufacturing skills such as upholstery, and the use of industrial lathes, presses, and routers. In consequence, many dozens of men found employment in industry, in support of the war effort. By now, the first female wartime St Dunstaners had been admitted.

In May 1943 the first blind POWs from Italian POW camps arrived home—five of whom were welcomed to St Dunstan's.[27] (Under the terms of the Geneva Convention, POWs who were unfit to fight were to be repatriated.)

In that year, on Fraser's initiative, the St Dunstan's Research and Development Department was created to address the requirements of St Dunstaners who were not only blind, but had lost, or lost the use of, one or both hands. The department would be run by Peter Nye, sergeant in the Royal Electrical and Mechanical Engineers, a man with normal vision but who, having been wounded, was slightly disabled himself. Innovations included the use of foot pedals to operate telephone switchboards, weaving looms, talking-book machines, carpentry tools—each fitted with a large ring to accommodate the forearm—and telephones with dials adapted to accommodate an artificial thumb, and which again, could be answered by the use of a foot pedal.

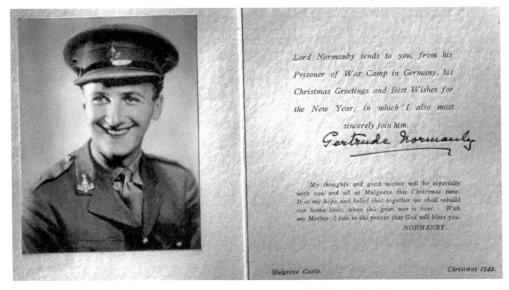

Lord Normanby sends to you, from his
Prisoner of War Camp in Germany, his
Christmas Greetings and Best Wishes for
the New Year, in which I also most
sincerely join him.

Gertrude Normanby

My thoughts and good wishes will be especially
with you and all at Mulgrave this Christmas time.
It is my hope and belief that together we shall rebuild
our home lives, when this grim war is over. With
my Mother, I join in the prayer that God will bless you.
NORMANBY.

Mulgrave Castle.   Christmas 1942.

Christmas card, 1942, sent by Gertrude Normanby on behalf of herself and her son, the Marquis of Normanby. The photograph of the Marquis was taken prior to June 1940 when he became a PoW in Germany. (*The Marquis of Normanby*)

Also in 1943, two more properties were acquired at Church Stretton: 'Belmont', which would provide accommodation for female blinded casualties of war, and 'Brockhurst', a former school which would not only provide extra accommodation, but also, with its swimming pool and 35 acres of land, offer excellent facilities for recreation and the construction of additional huts, including one to serve as a dance hall and another as a cafeteria. The impression gained is that, even though they had been relocated to a place almost 200 miles distant from their home at Ovingdean on the south coast, for St Dunstan's and St Dunstaners it was very much 'business as usual'!

In October 1943, Church Stretton gave a hero's welcome to twenty-seven blinded former POWs who had been released by the Germans from Kloster Haina. Included in their number was Lord Normanby (who now joined the Council of St Dunstan's and became an honorary member of its teaching staff), and Colonel Ansell, but not Major David Charters who 'had refused repatriation because he was the only British ophthalmologist in Germany and there were still seven blind prisoners of war [in that country]'. Three of these POWs were repatriated six months later, but Major Charters, even though 'he had been in captivity for over four years ... again refused [repatriation], and he stayed with the men until the end of the War'. He was subsequently awarded the MBE (Military Division), and received 'the lasting gratitude of St Dunstan's'.[28]

Colonel Ansell, however, was not among the St Dunstaners: 'I couldn't rightly be accepted as a St Dunstaner', he said, 'because I still had sufficient sight to get around'. However, 'I wanted to grow flowers', he said, and with Fraser's encouragement, he undertook a course of horticulture at Reading University.[29] Ansell subsequently created a flower farm at his home in Bideford, Devonshire, and went on to win a silver medal at the Chelsea Flower Show. In December of the next year, Ansell was elected Chairman of the British Showjumping Association.

In July 1944, St Dunstan's Hospital Unit was relocated to Stoke Mandeville Hospital in Buckinghamshire. Meanwhile in South Africa, the St Dunstan's Aftercare Committee continued to care for war-blinded South African servicemen, and in that year, St Dunstan's South Africa was registered as a company.

In 1945 the St Dunstan's Committee discussed whether to offer services to blinded Polish servicemen:

> [It was] decided unilaterally that blinded Polish servicemen should be treated as if they were British subjects. Later this position was regularized as the Council agreed with the proposal that, provided that the British Government allowed them stay in this country, eligible Polish and other Allied nationals should be given [i.e. offered] suitable training.[30]

In that year of 1945, the St Dunstan's Association for South African War-Blinded Veterans was founded. In March, the Blinded Servicemen's Trust Board was established as an independent unit by the Government of New Zealand to manage that country's branch of St Dunstan's. The scheme was originally established to cater for those who had served in the Second World War, but this was later extended to include all servicemen from the First World War to the Korean War and beyond.[31] Furthermore, a branch of St Dunstan's was opened in Auckland, principally through the efforts of two men, the aforementioned First World War St Dunstaner Donald McPhee, and James E. May.

An accountant by profession, James May served in the Middle East as lieutenant in the 25th Battalion, NZRB. On 16 December 1942, at Marble Arch, Libya (the Arch of the Philaeni, built by the occupying Italian colonists in 1937), he was severely injured when the truck in which he was travelling ran over an anti-tank mine. At the time the 2nd New Zealand Division was spearheading the Allied pursuit of the retreating Afrika Corps, following its defeat at the 2nd Battle of El Alamein. In the explosion, May was blinded and seriously injured.[32]

Having returned to New Zealand in May 1943 (May did not train at St Dunstan's, Regent's Park), May met Donald McPhee, representative for St Dunstan's in New Zealand. Together, they founded the New Zealand St Dunstan Blinded Servicemen's Association. It opened on 24 November 1945 at One Tree Hill, Epsom, Auckland, with McPhee as its first president and May as its first director and vice-president. (May also became Welfare Superintendent of the Royal New Zealand Foundation for the Blind.) St Dunstan's New Zealand would provide convalescence and training for all blinded and partially sighted servicemen returning from the Second World War, and long term care if need be. It was set up as a Trust, on which were representatives of the New Zealand Institute for the Blind, the Red Cross Society, the Order of St John of Jerusalem, St Dunstan's England, and the Commercial Travellers' and Warehousemen's Association Blinded Servicemen's Fund Trust Board.[33]

During the course of the Second World War, which ended in May 1945, in excess of 1,000 war-blinded men and women were admitted to St Dunstan's, including individuals from France, the Netherlands, Poland, Serbia, Estonia, and the USA. Forty-six were women.[34] Of the total, said Fraser, 'over 300 regained a useful degree of vision, and 100 had transferred to other institutions after treatment at our hospital. The remaining 600 would be St Dunstaners for the rest of their lives.'[34]

The Great Work Continues

In October 1945, St Dunstan's was informed by the Ministry of Health that of the POWs who would shortly be returning home, an estimated 300 had only limited vision, of whom 'about one-half will be unable to do work for which eyesight is essential'.[1] The men were examined by Robert C. Davenport, the resident ophthalmologist at St Dunstan's, with the following outcome:

> 11 were 'admitted to St Dunstan's or invited to Church Stretton for discussions about training; 2 were referred to the Scottish National Institute for the War Blind; 135 were listed to be followed up at varying intervals according to Davenport's assessment of the prospects of their remaining sight deteriorating further.[2]

Fraser also anticipated correctly (from the experience of the First World War) that men and women with long-term complications of wartime eye injuries would continue to experience problems for many years to come. In fact, many years later, on 2 December 1958, Fraser informed the House of Lords that mustard gas used by the Germans in the First World War was still causing blindness in British soldiers who had been exposed to it.[3]

Many prisoners of war returning from the Far East had endured deprivation, cruelty, and forced labour at the hands of the Japanese. Of these, some had become blind through injury, and others from the effects of malnutrition and beriberi (caused by a deficiency of vitamin B1—thiamine). Because this disease frequently causes neurological damage, sufferers had the added disadvantage of being unable to read Braille—having lost sensation in their fingers.

With the Germans, however, there were efforts to cooperate for the sake of the blinded on both sides. According to the *St Dunstan's Review*, during the (post-war) winter of 1945–46, Fraser, with the cooperation of Herr Voigt of Hamburg, helped to overcome 'the great political difficulties which stood in the way of re-constituting a German war-blind society'. (It will be recalled that Herr Hans Voigt had previously visited St Dunstan's in July 1937.) As a result the Military Government, British Zone of Military Occupation, Germany, 'approved the creation of the Society at that time called 'St Georg' which soon counted 4,000 members....' Furthermore, said Fraser, 'Friendship between our Chairman [Pearson] and Herr Voigt survived the war'.[4]

In 1946, St Dunstan's left Church Stretton and returned to Ovingdean. St Dunstaners currently numbered 1,673 from the First World War and 686 from the Second World War. British wartime leader Sir Winston Churchill attended St Dunstan's New Year Dance, where he presented Sir Ian Fraser with a new walking stick to commemorate twenty-five years as

Chairman. Sir Ian had lost his previous stick in 1944 in the Blitz, when his house had been damaged by enemy bombing.

Even for those with the worst injuries, every effort was made at St Dunstan's to provide mental and physical stimulation to lift depression and give the blinded men the will to lead independent lives. There were plenty of inspiring examples for St Dunstaners to follow. In 1947, St Dunstan's consultant ophthalmologist Robert Davenport undertook a second operation on Colonel Mike Ansell's eyes, but it was again unsuccessful. Said Ansell,

> [I] could just tell the difference between night and day. I was now accepted as a St Dunstaner and went to Avenue Road [St John's Wood, a home for officer St Dunstaners] to do my training and be 'rehabilitated'. I had already learned to type in Germany, and as for rehabilitation, that had been achieved the hard way, as a prisoner. However, St Dunstan's is a great regiment and I always feel proud to belong to it. In the week, the days were a routine, but that was easy for me: work in the morning, typewriting, Braille, the luncheon, and a walk in Regent's Park to feed the ducks. And as I moved around the lake, wondering vaguely if I might fall in, always I was thinking of how to put a sport, show-jumping, 'on the map'....[5]
>
> To me St Dunstan's has the traditions of a great regiment, and at times when I've been very down, I've only had to say, 'Thank the Good Lord I am a St Dunstaner' to feel two or three inches taller.[6]

Ansell, a former expert horseman and international polo player, would soon become familiar throughout the land through his association with the televised annual 'Horse of the Year Show' and other equestrian events which he enthusiastically promoted.

In the 1950s there were a range of activities organised for St Dunstaners to enjoy. In addition to dances organised by local branches, there were annual reunions, both in London

Colonel Sir Mike Ansell in 1979, with St Dunstan's welfare visitor, Yvonne Lyall. (*Blind Veterans UK*)

and elsewhere throughout the land—for example at Plymouth, Bristol, Belfast, Dublin, Luton, Cardiff, Manchester, Leeds, Glasgow, Bournemouth, Blackpool, Chester, Cardiff, and Ipswich. There were Bridge drives, including 'Harrogate Week'—an annual Bridge contest, held in the Yorkshire town; chess weekends; the Sir Arthur Pearson Memorial Competitions for darts, dominoes, and cribbage, for which trophies were awarded; annual outings to beauty spots such as Symonds Yat in Herefordshire, or to the seaside; an annual coach trip to Epsom races for the Derby, which was very popular; and the annual London to Brighton walk.

At Ovingdean, an annual Sports Day and Garden Party was held with Boy Scouts on hand to offer assistance. An annual Christmas Party was sponsored by the Grocers' Associations of Southern England (which, it will be remembered, had presented West House to St Dunstan's in 1918). The St Dunstan's Bridge Congress was also held at Ovingdean.

Every November, St Dunstaners were (and still are) among those who paraded at the Cenotaph in London. St Dunstaners also attended remembrance services held at their local war memorials and took part in the Festival of Remembrance, held by the Royal British Legion (founded in 1921) at London's Royal Albert Hall (Remembrance Sunday being the second Sunday in the month).

In August 1958 the *St Dunstan's Review* reminded its readers that 'every year [since 1945] fifty St Dunstaners have been invited to spend a week's holiday 'on board' H.M.S. *Daedalus* [Royal Naval Air Station, Lee-on-Solent, Hampshire] as guests of the Royal Navy. Nothing has ever been spared to give us a most wonderful welcome'.[7]

Finally, a large selection of books were available from the 'Talking Book Library'.

St Dunstan's had a truly global reach, as the experience of Alan John Dean clearly demonstrates. Alan was from Melbourne and born to Joseph Dean and his wife Mary. In July 1951 he enlisted in the Royal Australian Army. In February 1952 he was posted to Japan, where he became a member of the 3rd Royal Australian Regiment Support Group. The Korean War (25 June 1950–27 July 1953) was currently in progress, and the 3rd Regiment was serving with the Korean Force (or K-Force) in which some 17,000 Australians served. On 24 April 1952, at his Training Camp, twenty-year-old Alan was filling in a foxhole when he struck an unexploded US M69 training grenade. It burst on impact, and Alan was blinded and seriously wounded. This was two days prior to his regiment's proposed embarkation for Korea. He spent some time in hospital in Japan, and was then transferred to the Heidelberg Military Hospital, Melbourne, where he convalesced for about twelve months.

On 25 September 1953, Alan was admitted to St Dunstan's, Brighton:

It was a wonderful experience and one which I will never forget. I learned many things, not the least of which was to accept and adjust to my blindness.

As well as typing and Braille, Alan also learned weaving and other skills:

In the workshop I was introduced to simple engineering, mainly lathe work. Socially I enjoyed ballroom dancing at the Alan Dean School of Dancing [with which, by coincidence, he shared his name] in Brighton. I went to the theatre and cinemas many times. I had two special mates—Ray Wharton and Brian Judd.

Alan J. Dean, *c.* 1951. (*Patricia Dean*)

On his 'graduation', St Dunstan's presented Alan with a magnificent 'Ulmia' mitre-boxsaw. On his return to Australia, Alan worked for ten years for GM (General Motors) Holden Ltd at Fishermen's Bend, Victoria. He then studied for Adult Matriculation, and subsequently started up a home enterprise, making toys which he sold to kindergartens, child-minding centres, and private individuals.

On 6 April 1966, Alan married Patricia McDonald in Melbourne. Patricia worked for Guide Dogs for the Blind, Melbourne, and the couple met when Alan came to the centre to train with his guide dog—a boxer called 'Bo'.

Alan and Patricia had two sons. Said Patricia,

When it came to the toy-making, Alan had some wonderful designs and kept all the measurements in his head. He used an electric saw (very carefully) and other tools, and had a good range to help him with his work. I always kept away from him when he was using the electric saw, because he needed to concentrate.

He would assemble the toys and I would varnish them—one coat. Then Alan would sand them down and I would putty up any holes. Then I would put on the top coat. Alan and I worked as a team. He helped me and I helped him.

As for St Dunstan's, Patricia said,

While he was there he learned many things, 'not only hobbies and a trade but most importantly, how to be accepted by society as useful member'. And I think they did a great job. He used to have 'down' days, of course, and just needed to be left alone for a while.

Above: Alan J. Dean in his workshop at his family home in Melbourne. (*Patricia Dean*)

Right: Alan J. Dean and guide dog 'Bo' in training at the Guide Dog Centre, Melbourne. (*Patricia Dean*)

Above left: Alan J. Dean's St Dunstan's badge, representing his fifty years as a St Dunstaner. (*Patricia Dean*)

Above right: Alan J. Dean's St Dunstan's Australia badge. (*Patricia Dean*)

Left: Patricia Dean's St Dunstan's badge made of marcasite, such as were available for wives of St Dunstaners to purchase if they so wished. (*Patricia Dean*)

Emily Patricia Dean in February 1997,
aged eleven months, in a cart made by her
grandfather Alan J. Dean. (*Sharron Dean*)

In 1973 the family relocated to Western Australia. From 1987 to 1991, Alan served as President of the Blinded Soldiers of St Dunstan's, Western Australia. Patricia, for her part, subsequently served from 1995 to 2003 as the Association's honorary secretary/treasurer. Alan also served two terms as secretary/treasurer of the Federal Association. 'While he held office with the Blinded Soldiers Association,' said Patricia, 'I did most of the typing and he did the dictating! But he was the one with the good ideas and I carried out his instructions.'[8]

The following extract from an article in the *St Dunstan's Review*, dated June 1957, further demonstrates St Dunstan's' global reach:

> We have received two most interesting publications from the Malayan Association for the Blind, of which our St Dunstaner, Major D. R. Bridges, is Hon. Secretary. [David R. Bridges, an officer in the 7th Gurkha Rifles, was blinded in Burma in early 1945.]
>
> Major Bridges is Blind Welfare Officer for the Federation of Malaya. Magnificent work is being done by the Association and a blind girl has recently been placed as a telephone operator—the first blind girl in Malaya ever to be trained and placed in this profession. Major Bridges says that she is only one of several young Malayans for whom the future holds great hope.[9]

One of the greatest challenges for St Dunstan's was maintaining funds for aftercare. In the summer of 1958 (and on several subsequent occasions) Sir Ian Fraser, as an MP, fought for his St Dunstaners on two issues: first, 'the 10s. paid to a disabled ex-serviceman's wife, which had remained at that figure since 1919', and second, 'a very seriously disabled man receiving an unemployability allowance was allowed to earn as pocket money, or as payment for work which was in the nature of rehabilitation, a mere £1 per week'. Both these sums 'ought to

Alan J. Dean and his wife Patricia,
on their 40th wedding anniversary.
(*Patricia Dean*)

be raised,' he declared, and in respect of the latter, it was better that a man 'should have something to do rather than have nothing to do at all'.[10]

In late January 1956, Fraser and his wife Irene, representing St Dunstan's, reinforced ties abroad by visiting South Africa:

> [Sir Ian] opened the Attwell Garden for the Blind in Plein Square, Johannesburg. A number of St Dunstaners and their wives were present at the ceremony, which was attended by the Administrator of the Transvaal, Dr Nicoll, the Mayor of Johannesburg, Mr Leslie V. Hurd, as well as Reef Mayors and Mayoresses and Johannesburg City Councillors.
>
> At the entrance to the garden is a large gate, and on the pillars on either side is a cast bronze plaque bearing Sir Ian's name as the opener.

Also present was Mrs G. H. Beatty, President of St Dunstan's in Johannesburg. The Mayor of Johannesburg mentioned Fraser's long association with the city:

> This is not the first time that your name has been seen in Johannesburg; there are two streets called Fraser Street, one where your father [including Ian] and his family lived when you were a little boy, and the other where he had his office.[11]

Sir Ian Fraser (right) on his visit to Cape Town, January 1956. (*St Dunstan's South Africa*)

Fraser said he was very honoured that he had been asked to open the garden 'where there are specially chosen sweet-smelling herbs and flowers and comfortable seats and railings to show you the way, and no wheelbarrows to fall over, and quiet broken only by the sound of a fountain'.

A similar Garden for the Blind had recently been opened in Cape Town. Fraser said that those who, like himself, were 'keen on gardening may stoop down and feel the garden grow, and if he is skilful he may read the little label that is embossed in Braille, and remember the name so that he may put the plant in his own garden'.

Fraser was full of praise for the work of his organization in South Africa. 'Wherever you go', he said 'St Dunstan's is well known and respected, and in most places there is a St Dunstaner who contributes to our good report'.

In Maseru, capital of Basutoland, there was 'an active St Dunstan's Committee', and in Johannesburg there was 'a vigorous Committee'. In Cape Town, at the headquarters of St Dunstan's South Africa, Fraser had conferences with Sir Donald MacKenzie Kennedy, the Chairman. 'I attended a Board Meeting', he said, 'at which we discussed many matters of mutual interest. In the evening all St Dunstaners in the Cape Peninsula came to meet us at a reception.'[12]

In 1958, Ian Fraser was created a life peer and became Lord Fraser of Lonsdale. He now became involved in the development and testing of several scientific innovations. For example, the ultra-sonic torch mobility device, designed to warn the blind person of obstacles in his path as he or she moved around, and the Optacon reading device, 'with which, through a miniature television camera, a line of print can be scanned, letter by letter, so that the shape of each letter can be felt in a vibrating outline under the finger tips'.[13]

The September 1958 edition of *St Dunstan's Review* contained the following items of interest:

An order has been placed on behalf of Her Majesty Queen Elizabeth the Queen Mother, for two coconut fibre mats for Royal Lodge, Windsor.
   Many St Dunstaners will know of the beautiful model boats which St Dunstaner, George Fallowfield, makes from cigar boxes sent to him by Sir Winston Churchill.

Fallowfield, a private in the Royal Garrison Artillery, First World War, had been wounded in 1918 with a resultant loss not only of his sight but also of his hearing. He came to St Dunstan's in 1923.

An 85-year-old lady living in Acocks Green, Birmingham, also heard of them and … at her request he has modelled for her a perfect little wheelbarrow.

The *St Dunstan's Review* also mentioned recent headway made in publishing in Braille:

We are very pleased to bring to the attention of St Dunstaners the new 'Thistle' Book series now being published by the Scottish Braille Press. The books are all 'best sellers' in their own particular category and one new 'Thistle' book will be published each month.

Titles included, *My Story* by Matt Busby, *Anna Karenina* by Leo Tolstoy, *The Pursuit of Love* by Nancy Mitford, *Moonraker* by Ian Fleming, and *Doctor at Large* by Richard Gordon.[14]

On Christmas Day 1958 at 8.55 p.m., Fraser made the annual BBC broadcast for the 'Wireless for the Blind' fund.[15] The fund was founded in 1928 by St Dunstaner Ernest B. B. Towse VC, to provide wirelesses on loan to the blind or partially sighted.

Post-War Timeline of Events

In the decades following the Second World War, Britain and her allies would become involved in many new conflicts in such places as Palestine, Korea, Suez, East Africa, Malaya, Borneo, Aden, Cyprus, Northern Ireland, the Falkland Islands, the Middle East, and Afghanistan. St Dunstan's would continue to care not only for ex-servicemen and women who had been blinded in the two world wars, but also for those blinded thereafter, in the service of their country.

The following is a timeline of significant events related to St Dunstan's from the end of the Second World War to the present day.

1945: St Dunstan's admitted its youngest person: Michael Oliver, a thirteen-year-old boy who was blinded while on manoeuvres with the Air Training Corps.

1947: Sir Clutha MacKenzie was awarded the Kaisar-i-Hind gold medal for public service in India by King George VI. In that year Sir Neville succeeded his mother as President of St Dunstan's.

1948, February: Queen Elizabeth the Queen Mother paid her first visit to St Dunstan's, Ovingdean. A new administrative headquarters for St Dunstan's was established at No. 191, Old Marylebone Road, London (formerly Queen Charlotte's Hospital).

1950: 119 St Dunstaner physiotherapists were in practice: 68 from the First World War and 51 from the second.[1]

1952, 6 February: King George VI died and was succeeded by his daughter Queen Elizabeth II, who succeeded her father as Patron of St Dunstan's.

1953: The NIB became the Royal National Institute for the Blind (RNIB).

1956, June: A new headquarters for the CNIB was opened in Toronto.

1956, 9 December: A service to mark the 35th anniversary of Pearson's death was held at the St Dunstan's Chapel, Ovingdean, with the dedication of new stained-glass windows.

1957, June: A Braille reading contest was held at the National Library for the Blind, where St Dunstaners from Ovingdean were among the competitors. 'It was a particularly momentous occasion because Queen Elizabeth the Queen Mother was present'.[2]

1957, June: The aforementioned St Dunstaner Edward M. Brockie announced that the Braille watch, given to him by Pearson in 1916, was still keeping 'remarkably good time'.[3] West House was renamed Pearson House, in honour of Sir Arthur.

1959, 10 April: Lady Pearson died on in her ninetieth year. She was buried with Sir Arthur at Hampstead Cemetery.

1959, 12 November: Lord Fraser met with seventy-four blinded ex-servicemen and representatives from all states of the Commonwealth at Anzac House, Collins Street, Melbourne, during a tour of Australia.[4]

1961: Sir Neville's daughter Sally married actor Robert Hardy CBE.

1962, July: The Queen and Duke of Edinburgh visited Ovingdean.

1965: All St Dunstaners throughout the Commonwealth were presented with a mantle clock (with Braille inscription) to mark the 50th anniversary of the founding of St Dunstan's in 1915. Forty-seven years later, Alan Dean said of his clock 'has pride of place in our dining room, where it has stood for many years. It has always been most reliable (and admired), and every Saturday morning I wind it up. That is all that is required'.[5]

1965: By that year, '6,500 blinded soldiers, sailors and airmen, including a few women [had] passed through St Dunstan's or its associated societies in Commonwealth countries'.[6]

1965: Continuing the Pearson family's association with St Dunstan's, Sir Neville's son Nigel became a Member of its Council.

1966, June: St Dunstan's organized an International Conference on Sensory Devices for the Blind, held at the Great Western Royal Hotel, Paddington.

1971: To mark the 50th anniversary of Lord Fraser's Chairmanship, St Dunstan's, Ovingdean, was renamed 'Ian Fraser House'. By the early 1970s, St Dunstaners of the First World War currently numbered in excess of 400, and of the Second World War 'about twice as many'.[7]

1972: Pearson House (formerly West House) was rebuilt to include a new and fully equipped hospital wing for post-operative care. Convalescent care was also provided, and permanent residential accommodation for infirm, elderly, and bedridden St Dunstaners who had no home of their own.

Dudley Tregent, Australian First World War St Dunstaner with his granddaughter Eileen Frances Tregent, South Yarra, Melbourne, Australia, 1963. (*Eileen Crewes*)

Mantle clock (with Braille inscription), presented to Alan J. Dean in 1965 to mark the 50th anniversary of the founding of St Dunstan's in 1915. (*Patricia Dean*)

Braille inscription on top of clock, which translates, as stated, to 'St Dunstan's 1915–1965'. (*Patricia Dean*)

1973: The Australian Blinded Soldiers Association was renamed The Blinded Soldiers of St Dunstan's Australia.

1974, 19 December: Lord Fraser died having served as Chairman of St Dunstan's for fifty-three years. His ashes were interred in the cloisters of Westminster Abbey. He was succeeded by Ion Garnett-Orme.

1975: Among the guests at St Dunstan's annual reunion held at the Metropole Hotel, Brighton, was Mrs Natalie Opperman, Chairman of that organization's South African branch, together with approximately 250 St Dunstaners.

1975, 8 December: Nigel Pearson, the founder's grandson and Council Member, died aged fifty.

1976: St Dunstaners Tony Parkinson and Ray Peart competed in the Paralympic Games (then known as the 'Olympiad for the Physically Disabled') held in Toronto, Canada.

1977: St Dunstaners throughout the Commonwealth were presented with a copper rose bowl and a specially minted half-crown to mark Queen Elizabeth II's Silver Jubilee. In that year, Sir Neville resigned from the presidency of St Dunstan's and relocated to New Jersey, USA. He was succeeded as President by St Dunstaner and aforementioned Colonel Sir Michael Ansell CBE DSO DL (who in 1968 had received a knighthood).

1978, 18 March: Lady Fraser died.

1981: Sir Neville's wife, Lady Anne, died at Hightstown, New Jersey.

1982, 6 November: Sir Neville died aged eighty-three. His ashes, along with those of Lady Anne, were sent to England to be buried in London's Highgate Cemetery, where Neville's father Sir Arthur, his mother Ethel, and his son Nigel had also been interred.

1982: Terry Bullingham became the first casualty of the Falklands War to be admitted to St Dunstan's having been blinded while serving with the Royal Naval Air Service (RNAS) aboard HMS *Antrim*. After training and rehabilitation at Ovingdean, he was appointed Information Officer at the Fleet Air Arm Museum, RNAS, Yeovilton, Somerset. He subsequently became a technical officer for the blind. Terry's hobby was model engineering. He made, out of Meccano, a working replica of a steam engine and designed and produced a model crane—the full-sized version of which is in use in many dockyards today.

1983: Garnett-Orme retired and Admiral of the Fleet Sir Henry Leach, GCB, DL, succeeded him as Chairman of St Dunstan's.

1984: St Dunstan's once again moved its headquarters: this time to 12–14 Harcourt Street, London.

1985: The Queen and Duke of Edinburgh visited Ovingdean and formally opened the new South Wing of Ian Fraser House. It would be used specifically to accommodate St Dunstaners and their spouses.

1986: Colin Beaumont-Edmonds MC succeeded Colonel Sir Michael Ansell as President.

1990, 1 August: Her Majesty the Queen gave permission for a garden party to be held at Buckingham Palace to celebrate the 75th anniversary year of St Dunstan's. The finale was provided by Dame Vera Lynn, who sang wartime songs including: 'We'll Meet Again'.

1991: Three servicemen were admitted as casualties of the Gulf War.

1995: Pearson House was decommissioned and sold. Meanwhile, Ian Fraser House reverted to its original name of St Dunstan's, Ovingdean.

1996: A post-war St Dunstaner became the first blind person to reach the summit of Mont Blanc, the highest mountain in the Alps, via the First Classic Ascent Route.

1998: St Dunstan's, Ovingdean, was visited by the Duke of York. Captain Michael Gordon-Lennox succeeded Sir Henry Leach as Chairman.

2000: St Dunstan's amended its constitution so that support could be offered to former servicemen and women who had experienced loss of vision since retiring from the services.

2001, 15 May: The Queen and Duke of Edinburgh attended a reception at Buckingham Palace to commemorate St Dunstan's 85th anniversary year (which was actually the year previously, 2000).

2001: Stephen Menary, a fourteen-year-old army cadet who had been blinded in Northern Ireland by a booby-trapped torch, was admitted to St Dunstan's.

2003, October: The Duke of Kent visited Ovingdean.

2004: St Dunstaner Ray Hazan succeeded Colin Beaumont-Edmonds as President. A captain in the Royal Anglian Regiment, Hazan had been blinded in Northern Ireland in 1973 by an exploding parcel bomb. He also lost his right hand and sustained a considerable degree of hearing loss.

2005, 13 October: Three post-war St Dunstaners were made Freemen of the City of London. The ceremony took place at the Mansion House. A new residential centre for training and rehabilitation in the North of England was opened by St Dunstan's in Sheffield.

2006, May: Henry W. Allingham (born 6 June 1896) who had served with the Royal Naval Air Service during the First World War and whose eyesight was now failing, was admitted to St Dunstan's, Ovingdean. This was in the month prior to his 110th birthday.

Her Majesty The Queen opening new South Wing of Ian Fraser House in 1985. (*Blind Veterans UK*)

Above left: Captain Raymond L. Hazan OBE in 1978. (*Blind Veterans UK*)

Above right: William ('Billy') Baxter, 2 August 2003, when he successfully broke the land-speed record for a blind man on a motorcycle. Billy lost his sight in 1997 having contracted a virus while serving in Bosnia. (Billy is currently a member of Blind Veteran's' staff, based at Llandudno). (*Blind Veterans UK*)

Mark Threadgold (right) with instructor, 2002. Mark served as an electronics engineer with the Royal Corps of Signals. Years later, in 1999, he lost his sight in an accident which left him totally blind. (*Blind Veterans UK*)

Above left: Ray Sheriff who was blinded at the Battle of Arnhem in 1944. (*Blind Veterans UK*)

Above right: Captain Michael Gordon-Lennox, The Hon. Mrs Egerton-Warburton, and the author.

2007, June: The RNIB was renamed the Royal National Institute for Blind People.

2008: Major General Andrew Keeling succeeded Captain Michael Gordon-Lennox as Chairman.

2009, 18 July: St Dunstaner Henry Allingham, who for a month of his life was the world's oldest man, died peacefully at St Dunstan's, Ovingdean. He was buried with full military honours at St Nicholas' Church, Brighton.

2011: A new annexe was opened at the seaside resort of Llandudno in North Wales.

2012: The St Dunstan's organization was officially renamed 'Blind Veterans UK'. In recent years, many new avenues for recreation have opened up for blind veterans, for example, mountaineering in Snowdonia, skiing in European winter ski resorts, motorcycling, horseback riding, and water skiing.

2013, December: Timothy Davis succeeded Andrew Keeling as Chairman.

26 March each year: Founder's Day, where various awards are presented in memory of Sir Arthur Pearson. St Dunstan's, Regent's Park, opened for business on this date in 1915. One such award is the Ted Higgs Trophy for Lifetime Achievement (Higgs, a St Dunstaner, was blinded in 1944 while serving with the Royal Artillery), and in 2014, the recipient was Terry Bullingham.

Epilogue

For more than sixty years he has been blind
Behind that wall, these trees, with terrible
Longevity wheeled in the sun and wind
On pathways of the soldiers' hospital.

For half that time his story's troubled me—
That showroom by the ferry, where I saw
His basketwork, a touch-turned filigree
His fingers coaxed from charitable straw;

Or how he felt when young, enlisting at
Recruiting tables on the football pitch
To end up slumped across a parapet,
His eye-blood running in a molten ditch;

Or how the light looked when I saw two men,
One blind, one in a wheelchair, in that park,
Their dignity, which I have not forgotten,
Which helps me struggle with this lesser dark.

The war's too old for me to understand
How he might think, nursed now in wards of want,
Remembering that day when his right hand
Gripped on the shoulder of the man in front.

'War Blinded' by Douglas Dunn

Arthur Pearson lived his life in two parts: the first part in the world of the sighted, and the second part in the world of the blind. One may visualize him as a schoolboy at Winchester College—sociable, witty, popular, a good 'all-rounder'. Yet here, he was hit by a double misfortune: that of having to leave school prematurely due to his father being unable to afford the fees, and that of having to confront the fact that his eyesight was beginning to fail.

Nonetheless, by applying himself diligently, and by bringing his undoubted charm, talents, and energy to bear, he succeeded in founding two great enterprises: a publishing house, and the Fresh Air Fund for underprivileged children. He also leant invaluable support to Robert Baden-Powell's Scout Movement.

In his first life Pearson was a man of considerable achievement—educating and entertaining the nation with his newspapers and publishing empire. And yet, continuing from his first life into his second life there were common threads: his love of nature and the countryside; his enjoyment of horse-riding; and above all his humanity, compassion, and deep sense of social obligation.

In assessing the contribution made by Pearson to the world of the blind, it is pertinent to ask what would have been the fate of the blinded Allied soldiers, sailors, and airmen in the First World War had there been no St Dunstan's to assist them? The answer is an unhappy one, for, as already mentioned, they would have been sent straight home from hospital, and there to eke out a meagre existence on a pitifully inadequate pension supplied by a parsimonious and indifferent government; there to dwell among well-meaning relatives and friends, who would look after them inappropriately, and to whom they could not communicate their true feelings.

By 1914, Pearson's eyesight had deteriorated to the extent that, in the words of his son Sir Neville, he was 'unable to distinguish light from darkness'.[1] Yet he reacted positively, realizing that he was now in a unique position to assist men returning to Britain in increasing numbers, having been blinded in the First World War—and for two reasons. The first: prior to founding St Dunstan's he had worked for the NIB, and this experience would stand him in good stead. The second: being blind himself, he had a far better insight into the mind of a blinded person than a sighted person could ever have.

Finally, Pearson felt a strong sense of obligation to these men on account of the sacrifice that they had made. This is apparent in the foreword to his book *Victory Over Blindness*, in which he dedicates the volume not only to his immediate colleagues, but to the 'innumerable kindly and sympathetic folk [who] have helped in a thousand ways to make the men at St Dunstan's happy, to repay, as best might be done, the debt which is owed to them'.[2] And again, in the final chapter of *Victory over Blindness*, he declares,

> All that was done at St Dunstan's was a tribute to the soldiers blinded in the war, some recognition of what was owed to them, the most practical form of sympathy that could be offered, an expression of gratitude.[3]

Now, all the determination which he had shown in building his publishing empire would be channelled into his new project, St Dunstan's. In fact, so determined was Pearson to achieve 'Victory Over Blindness'—not only for himself but for others—that some might say he was in denial about his own condition. Said Neville,

> He would have his blind men talked to of things seen, so that they could make mental pictures of them. When taking his escort—he did the taking—for a walk near Bourne End [where his home was], he would stop to point out this laburnum tree or that prospect over the river. He refused to recognize his own disability.[4]

What was the source of Pearson's motivation? Was he a Christian? After all, his father (who died in 1916) was a Church of England clergyman, as his grandfather had been. And the family motto was '*In Deo Spes*'—'In God is my Hope'.

It has to be said that Pearson makes very few references to Christianity in his book *Victory Over Blindness*. However, it does contain one very significant statement, where he refers to a seat situated under the mulberry tree on the lawn at St Dunstan's: 'If you look on the back of the seat as you rise from it, you will see these words are written,' and he quotes the following lines:

> The kiss of the sun for pardon,
> The song of the birds for mirth,
> You're nearer to God in a garden
> Than anywhere else on Earth.

Pearson's success was due to the fact that he treated his men both humanely and in a holistic way—defined as 'the treating of the whole person including mental and social factors, rather than just the symptoms of a disease'.[5] In so doing, he changed the attitude of the general public completely, not only towards his St Dunstaners, but also towards blind people in general.

On the occasion of Pearson's funeral, Queen Alexandra, St Dunstan's' patron, sent a wreath. This contained a message summarizing the Chief's life, appositely and succinctly, with a quotation from US physician and poet Edward Hazan Parker:[6]

> Life's race well run,
> Life's work well done,
> Life's crown well won.
> Now comes rest.

> from Alexandra.

Pearson's other great legacy, the *Daily Express* newspaper, continues to flourish. Not only that, its current proprietor Richard Desmond is passionately concerned with the welfare of the blind. To this end, he donated the sum of £2.5 million to London's Moorfields Eye Hospital NHS Foundation Trust. The result was the opening of the Richard Desmond Children's Eye Centre by Her Majesty the Queen on 23 February 2007. On that occasion Sir Thomas Boyd-Carpenter, the hospital's Chairman, uttered words which would have gladdened Pearson's heart:

> Moorfields includes the largest concentration of ophthalmologists anywhere in the world. Children represent a very important part of our work.

To this day, Pearson's many descendants, by their work on behalf of the sick and the needy, continue to keep the flame of the torch that he lit burning brightly.

In 2015, Blind Veterans UK's centenary year, it is interesting to reflect how things have changed. From 1915 onwards, every St Dunstaner was presented with a Braille watch as a first step towards independence, while today, 'talking watches, document-reading scanners and specially designed computers help them take charge of their own lives, without being reliant on others'. It is the proud boast of Blind Veterans UK that,

> Since we were founded 100 years ago, we have helped more than 33,000 blind veterans regain their independence, rebuild their confidence and start living their lives once more.

And, without doubt, there is a continuing need for Blind Veterans UK in these present times:

> Today, we are helping more blind veterans than at any point in our history. This year (2015), we are expecting 850 more to turn to us for the first time.

In fact, this centenary year of 2015 sees the launch of Blind Veterans UK Centenary Appeal. It also sees the launch of three important initiatives:

• Young Veterans Empowerment Programme'. This is designed to give training and employment advice, thereby getting the person back to work and enabling him or her to support themselves and any family they may have.

• 'Life Skills for Independent Living Programme'. To help 'the most vulnerable veterans struggling with their sight loss, learn the life skills needed to live on their own without

Centenary birthday greetings, featuring blind veterans Jim Hartley and Paul Jacobs. (*Blind Veterans UK*)

relying on others to care for them. To do this, we are developing part of out Llandudno centre to create purpose-built apartments where they can live and learn through intensive one-to-one training with our dedicated programme staff, before taking the next step to moving into their own homes.'

- 'Get Out and Live (G.O.A.L)'. This is an initiative for older veterans. 'Throughout the coming year, we will be organizing a series of events—from reunions to remembrance services—which older veterans can enjoy as a group. Bringing them together through this club, helps them share their bond of Service and of blindness—a connection you simply cannot get anywhere else.'

Appendices

I: St Dunstan

St Dunstan was born at Glastonbury in Somerset in 924, where, legend has it, a church had been founded in the first century by St Joseph of Arimathea (a disciple of Jesus Christ) who had brought with him the Holy Grail. This church became Glastonbury Abbey, built by the Benedictine order of monks between the tenth and eleventh centuries.

Having been educated at Glastonbury Abbey, Dunstan took monastic vows. In 945, he was appointed Abbot of Glastonbury by King Edmund and set about renovating the abbey and establishing it as a centre of religious teaching. Dunstan went on to become Bishop of Worcester, then of London, and finally, in 961, Archbishop of Canterbury. His Feast Day is 19 May.

II: Louis Braille

At the age of ten, Braille was sent to a school for blind boys in Paris, to be taught practical skills, such as applying cane to chairs and making slippers. The boys were also taught to read, by feeling letters which had been embossed on the surface of the page, but not to write. This method was soon to be superseded however. In 1821, a soldier Charles Barbier, visited the school and demonstrated a system which he had invented. It was called 'night writing', and it enabled soldiers to pass instructions along a trench at night without having to speak, thereby not giving their positions away. It consisted of twelve raised dots which could be arranged to represent different sounds. Braille realized what a valuable tool this was, but not in its present form. He therefore reduced the number of dots to six, and experimented for several years in order to develop the codes necessary for the dots to represent the written word. He also developed similar codes for mathematics and music.

Braille eventually became a teacher at the school at which he had been a student. His system was later widely adopted throughout the world, but he did not live to see this, for he died of tuberculosis in 1852 at the age of only forty-two.

III: Pearson's Legacy in Charities and Businesses

Blind Veterans UK Today: The national charity continues to provide crucial assistance to blind ex-servicemen and women and their families. Blind veterans are offered lifelong support which enables them to regain their independence, meet new challenges, and achieve a better quality of life.

The Royal National Institute for the Blind: To this day, the Pearson Staff Memorial Benefit Fund seeks to alleviate need among RNIB staff and former staff members.

The Fresh Air Fund: Launched by Pearson in 1892, The Fresh Air Fund's name was changed in 1981 to 'Pearson's Holiday Fund'. With The Queen as its patron, it is still helping poor, needy, and disadvantaged children to enjoy a holiday in Britain.

The Daily Express: Continues to this day as a flourishing newspaper.

IV: Royal Patrons of St Dunstan's

1915–25, Queen Alexandra
1925–36, No patron
1936, Edward VIII
1936–52, George VI
1952 to date, Elizabeth II

V: Chairmen of St Dunstan's

1915–21, Sir Arthur Pearson Bt, GBE
1921–74, Lord Fraser of Lonsdale, CH, CBE
1975–83, Ion Garnett-Orme, CBE
1983–98, Admiral of the Fleet Sir Henry Leach, GCB, DL
1998–2008, Captain Michael Gordon-Lennox, RN
2008–13, Major General Andrew Keeling, CB, CBE
2013–present, Timothy Davis

VI: Presidents of St Dunstan's

1921–47, Lady Pearson, DBE
1947–77, Sir Neville Pearson Bt
1977–86, Colonel Sir Michael Ansell, CBE, DSO, DL
1986–2004, Colin Beaumont-Edmonds, MC
2004–present, Raymond Hazan

VII: Pearson Family Tree

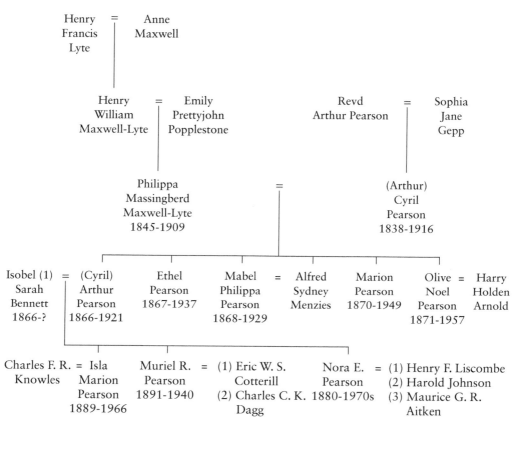

On 14 June 1921, Mrs Anne Spaulding (née Davis) of New York City (whom he later married
— see below) bore Neville a daughter, Shirley Davis Spaulding.

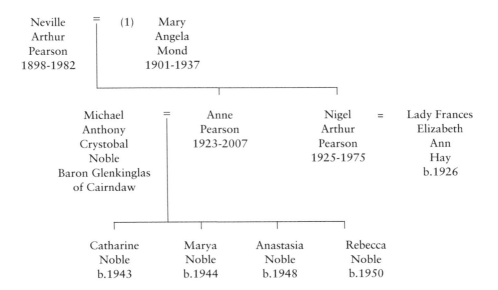

```
Neville          =    (1)    Mary
Arthur                       Angela
Pearson                      Mond
1898-1982                    1901-1937
         ┌─────────────────────────┬──────────────────────┐
    Michael         =    Anne              Nigel      =    Lady Frances
    Anthony              Pearson           Arthur          Elizabeth
    Crystobal            1923-2007         Pearson         Ann
    Noble                                  1925-1975       Hay
    Baron Glenkinglas                                      b.1926
    of Cairndaw
       ┌──────────┬────────────┬──────────┐
    Catharine   Marya      Anastasia   Rebecca
    Noble       Noble      Noble       Noble
    b.1943      b.1944     b.1948      b.1950
```

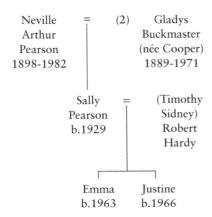

```
Neville          =    (2)    Gladys
Arthur                       Buckmaster
Pearson                      (née Cooper)
1898-1982                    1889-1971
         Sally         =    (Timothy
         Pearson            Sidney)
         b.1929             Robert
                            Hardy
            ┌──────────┐
         Emma       Justine
         b.1963     b.1966
```

```
Neville      =    (3)    Anne Elebash,
Arthur                   formerly Spaulding,
Pearson                  née Davis
1898-1982                1898-1982
```

Endnotes

Chapter 1: Arthur Pearson: Early Life

1. Ethel Pearson evidently did not marry. Mabel Pearson married Reverend Alfred S. Menzies in 1891, and the couple had a daughter, Helen Joyce Menzies. Olive Pearson married Harry H. Arnold, manufacturer of bricks and pottery.
2. Winchester College, a public—which in England means private—school.
3. Obituary, Cyril Arthur Pearson, *The Wykehamist*, 13 February 1922.
4. *Ibid.*
5. *Ibid.*
6. Dark, Sidney, *The Life of Sir Arthur Pearson*, p. 26.
7. *Ibid.*
8. Pearson, Sir Arthur, 'My Early Days with Titbits'.
9. *Ibid.*
10. *Ibid.*
11. Dark, *op. cit.*, p. 37.
12. *Ibid.*, p 26.
13. *Ibid.*, p. 42.
14. Nora Pearson was married three times: to publisher Henry F. Lipscomb in 1912, who she divorced in 1925; then to Harold Johnson in 1926, who she divorced in 1933; and finally to Maurice G. R. Aitken in 1934. Nora spent her latter years in Bombay as a member of various social welfare organisations. In 1954 she was awarded the MBE (Member of the Order of the British Empire).

Chapter 2: *Pearson's Weekly*

1. *St Dunstan's Review*, in Heasman, p. 11.
2. Sir Neville Pearson, 1958. Article written about his late father for the Scout Movement, in Heasman, pp. 42-3.
3. Pearson subsequently moved several more times to other properties in Surrey: 'Round Down', Gomshall (1891); 'Cattershall Manor', Godalming (1895); and 'Broadwater', Godalming (1896).

Chapter 3: Pearson's Fresh Air Fund

1. Heasman, Robert, 'Who was Cyril Arthur Pearson?' pp. 3, 39.
2. *Ibid.*, pp.21-2.
3. *Ibid.*, pp. 21-22, 24.

Chapter 4: Pearson Remarries: Frensham Place

1. *St Dunstan's Review*, in Heasman, p. 11.
2. Dark, Sidney, *The Life of Sir Arthur Pearson*, p. 7.
3. *This England*, in Heasman, p. 12.

Chapter 5: Pearson the Newspaper Proprietor

1. Parker, Eric, *Hesketh Prichard*, pp. 45-6.
2. Gotto, Basil, *Memoir*, pp. 151-2.
3. *New York Times*, 14 June 1901.
4. Information kindly supplied by Doreen Birks. *Bradshaw's Continental Railway Guide* was published by cartographer, publisher, and printer George Bradshaw, 1800-53—the first edition of which appeared in 1847.

Chapter 6: Pearson and the Search for the Giant Sloth

1. The megatherium is a relation of the mylodon, or small ground sloth which exists today.
2. Prichard, Hesketh V. H., *Through the Heart of Patagonia*, p. xii.
3. The Hunterian Museum, named after Scottish physiologist and surgeon John Hunter.
4. Prichard, *op. cit.*, Appendix B.

Chapter 7: C. Arthur Pearson Ltd

1. *The Concise Oxford Dictionary*.

Chapter 8: Pearson and the Scout Movement

1. Everett, Sir Percy, *The First Ten Years*, p. 8.
2. *Ibid.*, p. 8.
3. Baden-Powell, Robert S. S., *Scouting for Boys*, Appendix.
4. Everett, *op. cit.*, p. 11.
5. Pearson to Hesketh V.H. Prichard, 26 May 1912, in Eric Parker's *Hesketh Prichard*, p. 120.

Chapter 9: Pearson and the National Institute for the Blind

1. Dark, Sidney, *The Life of Sir Arthur Pearson*, p. 218.
2. *Ibid.*, p. 143.
3. *Ibid.*, pp.144-45.
4. *Ibid.*, p. 140.

Chapter 10: Pearson and the Founding of St Dunstan's

1. 'Minutes of Blinded Soldiers & Sailors Care Committee' (*Minutes*), 29 January 1915 to 12 December 1921.
2. *Minutes.*
3. Pearson, Sir Arthur, 'St Dunstans: The Story of the Blinded Soldiers of the British Army'.
4. Pearson, Sir Arthur, *Victory Over Blindness*, p. 25.
5. *Ibid.*, pp. 57-8.
6. *Ibid.*, p. 12.
7. *Ibid.*, p. 11.
8. Dark, Sidney, *The Life of Sir Arthur Pearson*, p. 156.
9. *Minutes.*
10. *Ibid.*
11. *Ibid.*
12. *Ibid.*
13. *Ibid.* The significance of the word 'travellers' is not known.
14. *Ibid.*
15. *Ibid.*
16. *Ibid.*
17. *Ibid.*

18. The clock was famously mentioned in several works of English literature, including *Fortunes of Nigel* by Sir Walter Scott, *A Tale of Two Cities* by Charles Dickens, *The Warden* by Anthony Trollope, and in several poems by William Cowper. It was returned to the church in Fleet Street in 1935.
19. Pearson, Sir Arthur, *Victory Over Blindness*, p. 54.

Chapter 11: The Newcomer to St Dunstan's

1. Lawson, Sir Arnold, *War Blindness at St Dunstan's*, p. 129.
2. Pearson, Sir Arthur, *Victory Over Blindness*, pp. 68-70.
3. Sir Arthur Pearson, speech made at Baltimore, Maryland, USA, Friday 17 January 1919.
4. Pearson, *op. cit.*, pp. 35-36.
5. Hall, (Joseph) Rex, *The World is Mine*, p. 47. Hall served in the First World War and was an Army Commander in the Second World War. He subsequently became Director of Rehabilitation for the Australian Army and for forty-five years was honorary secretary and chairman of the Victorian Blinded Soldier's Welfare Trust. Hall was a very close friend of St Dunstaner Dudley Tregent for over fifty years.
6. *Ibid.*, p. 47.
7. Pearson, Sir Arthur, 'St Dunstans: The Story of the Blinded Soldiers of the British Army'.
8. *Ibid.*
9. *Ibid.*
10. White sticks had not yet come into use.
11. Dark, Sidney, *The Life of Sir Arthur Pearson*, p. 166.
12. Fraser of Lonsdale, Lord, *My Story of St Dunstan's*, p. 37.
13. Castleton, D., *Blind Man's Vision*, p. 21, and *St Dunstan's: A Story of Accomplishment*, p. 2.

Chapter 12: St Dunstan's Goes from Strength to Strength

1. Pearson, Sir Arthur, *Victory Over Blindness*, p. 23.
2. *Minutes.*
3. *Ibid.*
4. *Ibid.*
5. *Ibid.*
6. *Ibid.*
7. Pearson, *op. cit.*, p. 38.
8. *Minutes.*
9. *Ibid.*
10. *Ibid.*
11. *Ibid.*
12. *Ibid.*
13. *Ibid.*
14. *Ibid.*
15. *Ibid.*
16. *Ibid.*
17. Fraser of Lonsdale, Lord, *My Story of St Dunstan's*, p. 36.
18. *Ibid.*
19. *Ibid.*
20. *Ibid.*
21. *Ibid.*
22. *St Dunstan's Review*, September 1916.
23. Pearson, *op. cit.*, p. 38.
24. *Minutes.*
25. *Ibid.*
26. Pearson, *op. cit.*, p. 27.
27. Prichard, Hesketh V. H., *Sniping in France*, pp. 110-14.

28. *Minutes.*
29. *Ibid.*
30. *Ibid.* Captain Ward has not been identified.
31. *Ibid.*
32. *Ibid.*

Chapter 13: Types of Eye Injury and their Treatment

1. Pearson, Sir Arthur, *Victory Over Blindness*, p. 13.
2. Ormond, Arthur W., 'A Report on the Ophthalmic Work carried out at the 2nd London General Hospital', St Mark's College, Chelsea, 1914–19, p. 3.
3. *Ibid.*, p. 6.
4. Lawson, Sir Arnold, *War Blindness at St Dunstan's*, p. 136.
5. *Ibid.*, p. 35.
6. Ormond, *op. cit.*, pp. 12-13.
7. *Ibid.*, pp. 36, 38, 41.
8. Article 23 of The Hague Convention IV of 18 October 1907 (a convention respecting the laws and customs of war on land) came into force on 26 January 1910. Signed by virtually all the major European powers, it declared that 'It is especially forbidden … to employ poison or poisoned weapons.'
9. Ormond, *op. cit.*, p. 11.
10. 'The St Dunstan's Institute' by Greville Robins in *Saint Dunstan's Annual*, 1935. London: S.C.S., Gower Street.
11. Ormond, *op. cit.*, p. 14.
12. *Ibid.*, p. 7.
13. *Ibid.*, p. 8.
14. Lawson, *op. cit.*, p. 47.
15. Dark, Sidney, *The Life of Sir Arthur Pearson*, p. 159.

Chapter 14: Pearson's Brainchild in Operation

1. Pearson, Sir Arthur, *Victory Over Blindness*, pp. 120-21.
2. Fraser of Lonsdale, Lord, *My Story of St Dunstan's*, p. 116.
3. Hall, (Joseph) Rex, *The World is Mine*, p. 46.
4. Pearson, *op. cit.*, pp. 125-26.
5. *Ibid.*, p. 123.
6. Sir Arthur Pearson, speech made at Baltimore, Maryland, USA, Friday 17 January 1919.
7. Hall, *op. cit.*, p. 46.
8. Sir Arthur Pearson, speech made at Baltimore, Maryland, USA, Friday 17 January 1919.
9. Fraser, *op. cit.*, p. 134.
10. Information kindly supplied by Margaret Berryman.
11. *Hawera & Normanby Star*, Southern Taranaki, New Zealand, 10 March 1906.
12. Fraser, *op. cit.*, p. 58.
13. *Ibid.*, p. 123.
14. Sir Arthur Pearson, speech made at Baltimore, Maryland, USA, Friday 17 January 1919.
15. Pearson, *op. cit.*, pp. 166-67.
16. *Ibid.*, p. 43.
17. *Ibid.*, pp. 168-69.
18. Fraser, *op. cit.*, p. 46.
19. Sir Arthur Pearson, speech made at Baltimore, Maryland, USA, Friday 17 January 1919.
20. *The Times*, 21 January 1947. Sir Arnold Lawson's Obituary.
21. Sir Arthur Pearson, speech made at Baltimore, Maryland, USA, Friday 17 January 1919.
22. Pearson, *op. cit.*, p. 117.
23. *Ibid.*, pp. 48-49.

24. Sir Arthur Pearson, speech made at Baltimore, Maryland, USA, Friday 17 January 1919.
25. Dark, *op. cit.*, pp. 164-65.
26. Sir Arthur Pearson, speech made at Baltimore, Maryland, USA, Friday 17 January 1919.
27. Pearson, *op. cit.*, p. 193.
28. Obituary, Cyril Arthur Pearson, *The Wykehamist*, 13 February 1922.
29. Sir Arthur Pearson, speech made at Baltimore, Maryland, USA, Friday 17 January 1919.
30. Pearson *op. cit.*, pp. 205-7.
31. Fraser, *op. cit.*, p. 166.
32. *Ibid.*, p. 160.
33. Sir Arthur Pearson, speech made at Baltimore, Maryland, USA, Friday 17 January 1919.
34. Pearson, *op. cit.*, p. 167.
35. *Ibid.*, p. 317.
36. Sir Arthur Pearson, speech made at Baltimore, Maryland, USA, Friday 17 January 1919.
37. Dark, *op. cit.*, p. 168.
38. Pearson, *op. cit.*, p. 299.
39. *Ibid.*, pp. 280-81.

Chapter 15: Aftercare

1. Dark, Sidney, *The Life of Sir Arthur Pearson*, p. 16.
2. Fraser of Lonsdale, Lord, *My Story of St Dunstan's*, Fraser, p. 53.
3. Dark, *op. cit.*, pp. 173-74.
4. *Ibid.*, pp. 183-91.
5. St Dunstan's *Annual Report* for year ending March 1920.
6. *Ibid.*, pp. 180-81.

Chapter 16: Gladys Cooper and St Dunstan's

1. Cooper, Gladys, *Gladys Cooper*, pp. 19, 28.
2. *Ibid.*, pp. 157-58.
3. *Ibid.*, p. 157.
4. Gladys was as good as her word. She was present, for example, on 23 June 1931, when the Duke of Kent (later King George VI) joined celebrations in Epping Forest, Essex, marking the fortieth year of the Fund.
5. Information kindly supplied by Marya Egerton-Warburton.

Chapter 17: Pearson and the Secret of His Success

1. Fraser, Lord of Lonsdale, *My Story of St Dunstan's*, pp. 67-68.
2. Pearson, Sir Arthur, *Victory Over Blindness*, pp. 296-97.
3. Fallowfield, George, 'Who designed the St. Dunstan's badge, and its colours?' *St Dunstan's Review*, April 1943.
4. Pearson, *op. cit.*, p. 118.
5. *Ibid.*, pp. 60-61.
6. *Ibid.*, p. 318.
7. *Ibid.*, p. 319.
8. Fraser, *op. cit.*, p. 169.
9. Pearson, *op. cit.*, pp. 13-14.
10. Fraser, *op. cit.*, pp. 116-18.
11. Pearson, *op. cit.*, p. 14.
12. Fraser, *op. cit.*, p. 55.
13. Pearson, *op. cit.*, p. 52.
14. *Ibid.*, pp. 55-56.
15. Fraser, *op. cit.*, p. 54.

16. Lawson, Sir Arnold, *War Blindness at St Dunstan's*, p. 111.
17. Fraser, *op. cit.*, p. 68.
18. *Ibid.*, p. 70.
19. 'Martial Sentiment', *Chronicles of the NZEF*, 3 no. 33 (1917): 207.
20. Information kindly supplied by Jean Norman (née Waldin).
21. Lawson, *op. cit.*, p. 130.
22. Dark, Sidney, *The Life of Sir Arthur Pearson*, p. 159.

Chapter 18: The 'Chief' visits the Front

1. *New York Times*, 16 February 1922. Neville A. Pearson, Royal Field Artillery, commissioned 2nd Lieutenant, 17 June 1917. Dates for Neville Pearson at Eton College kindly supplied by Eleanor Cracknell, college archivist.
2. Report of an account given by Sir Arthur Pearson of his recent visit to the Front.
3. Dark, Sidney, *The Life of Sir Arthur Pearson*, p. 176.

Chapter 19: More Developments at St Dunstan's

1. *Minutes.*
2. Fraser of Lonsdale, Lord, *My Story of St Dunstan's*, p. 20.
3. *Ibid.*, p. 50.
4. Dark, Sidney, *The Life of Sir Arthur Pearson*, p. 139.
5. *Minutes.*
6. *St Dunstan's Review*, February and March 1918.
7. *Minutes.*
8. *Ibid.*
9. *New York Times*, 21 March 1918.
10. *The Times*, 'A Symbol of Union', 27 May 1918.
11. *Minutes.* Mr Mayer has not been identified.
12. *Minutes.*
13. *Ibid.*
14. *St Dunstan's Review*, April 1957.
15. Castleton, D., *Blind Man's Vision*, pp. 21-22.

Chapter 20: The Armistice and Beyond

1. *St Dunstan's Review*, July 1940.
2. Dark, *op. cit.*, p. 176.
3. Pearson, Sir Arthur, *Victory Over Blindness*, Pearson, pp. 31-32.
4. Sir Arthur Pearson, speech made at Baltimore, Maryland, USA, Friday 17 January 1919.
5. *Minutes.*
6. *Ibid.*
7. *Ibid.*
8. *Ibid.*
9. *Daily Mirror*, July 1919.
10. Fraser of Lonsdale, Lord, *My Story of St Dunstan's*, p. 208.
11. *Minutes.*
12. *Ibid.*
13. *Ibid.*
14. *Ibid.*
15. *Ibid.*
16. *Ibid.*
17. *Ibid.*
18. *Ibid.*

Chapter 21: Some British St Dunstaners

1. *The London Gazette*, 26 September 1916.
2. Angus Buchanan died on 1 March 1944 and is buried at Coleford Cemetery.
3. Information kindly supplied by the Gordon Highlanders Museum, Aberdeen.
4. St Dunstan's Review, 1971–72, p. 65.

Chapter 22: Some St Dunstaners from Overseas

1. Edwin Albert Baker, Service Record, Library and Archives, Canada.
2. Information kindly supplied by Blind Veterans UK.
3. Edwin A. Baker died on 7 April 1968.
4. Harris Turner, Service Record, Library and Archives, Canada.
5. Fraser of Lonsdale, Lord, *My Story of St Dunstan's*, p. 197.
6. *Ibid.*, p. 199.
7. Information kindly supplied by Blind Veterans UK and Library and Archives Canada.
8. Routh, S. J., 'Scrymgeour, James Tindal Stuart (1885–1965)', *Australian Dictionary of National Biography*, Volume 16, 2002.
9. Hall, (Joseph) Rex, *The World is Mine*, Hall, pp. 45-46.
10. *Ibid.*, p. 47.
11. *Ibid.*, p. 47.
12. *Ibid.*, p. 47.
13. Information kindly supplied by Blind Veterans UK and by Eileen Crewes, granddaughter of Dudley Crewes.
14. Fraser, *op. cit.*, p. 204.
15. Wooller, Frank C., 'The History of the Blinded Soldiers of St Dunstan's Australia'.
16. Fraser, *op. cit.*, p. 201.
17. Catran, Ken, and Penny Hansen, *Pioneering A Vision: A History of the Royal New Zealand Foundation for the Blind*, pp. 43-44.
18. Information kindly provided by NZDF Personnel and Medals.
19. *St Dunstan's Review*, 2 February 1918.
20. Catran, *op. cit.*, p. 199. Information kindly supplied by Alison Jones and Blind Foundation New Zealand.
21. *St Dunstan's Review*, June 1921.
22. *From Light in Darkness: A Brief History of the Jubilee Institute for the Blind: A Record of Great Achievements*. 1928. Auckland, New Zealand: Jubilee Institute for the Blind. Also from information supplied by Cyril Jenkin, early leader of The Commercial Travellers' and Warehousemen's Association of New Zealand, courtesy Theo V. Thomas, pp. 279, 210-11.
23. *St Dunstan's Review*, May 1940.
24. Sir Thomas Mackenzie's daughters Mary and Helen also worked for the NZWCA for almost three years as volunteers. Helen served as a member of the organising committee, and was Honorary Secretary of the Hospitality Committee, later called the Hospital Comforts Committee.
25. Tripp, L. O. H., 'War Relief and Patriotic Societies' in *The War Effort of New Zealand*, H. T. B. Drew, (editor), Auckland: Whitcombe and Tombs, 1932, p. 185.
26. Lance Corporal A. L. Williams—believed not to have been a war-blinded St Dunstaner.
27. Carr, Carolyn Jane, 'A Most Creditable Production'.
28. *Ibid.*
29. Clutha Mackenzie, *Writings by Clutha Nantes Mackenzie*, Unpublished Typescript, Chapter 13, p. 18. Held by his grand-daughter Mrs R. Cole-Baker.
30. Mackenzie, Trooper Clutha, New Zealand Mounted Rifles, *Union Annual for South Africa*, p. 52, September 1922.
31. 'Future of blind soldiers: Mr Mackenzie's charge', *New Zealand Herald* LVI(17213): 9; 15 July 1919.
32. New Zealand's Jubilee Institute for the Blind was founded in 1891 in Parnell, Auckland, with funds in 1887 during celebrations for Queen Victoria's Golden Jubilee.

33. *St Dunstan's Review*, March 1990.
34. Fraser, *op. cit.*, p. 279.
35. *Ibid.*, pp. 210-11.

Chapter 23: Pearson and Helen Keller

1. Information supplied by Helen Keller International.
2. Keller, Helen Adams, *The Story of My Life*, p. 10.
3. *Ibid.*, p. 30.
4. *Ibid.*, p. 41.
5. *Ibid.*, p. 57.
6. Helen Keller, speech at the Carnegie Hall, New York City, 5 January 1916.
7. Dark, Sidney, *The Life of Sir Arthur Pearson*, pp. 196-200.

Chapter 24: Richard King Huskinson

1. Pearson, Sir Arthur, *Victory Over Blindness*, pp. 309-10, 314.

Chapter 25: Death of the 'Chief'

1. Anne Davis (1898–1981), daughter of businessman Daniel Webster Davis of Conemaugh, Pennsylvania, and his wife Elda (née Dunmire). In 1928, Anne and her husband Chester Warren Spaulding divorced. In November of that year she married Baisley Powell Elebash, who she divorced in 1935. *New York Times*, 10 December 1943.
2. *The Times*, 12 December 1921.
3. *Ibid.*
4. Dark, Sidney, *The Life of Sir Arthur Pearson*, p. 203.
5. *Minutes.*
6. Lady Pearson also served from 1922 until her death in 1959 as Vice-President of the RNIB.
7. On 18 January 1922, Sir Neville Pearson replaced his late father as President of the Fresh Air Fund, and Lady Pearson became a Trustee and Member of its Council.
8. In his time, Fraser would also serve as President of the Royal British Legion and Governor of the BBC for two terms.
9. *Minutes.*
10. *The Times*, 14 December 1921.
11. 'Blindness as an Opportunity', *The Times*, 14 December 1921.
12. Dark, *op. cit.*, pp. 205-17.
13. Baden-Powell, Robert S. S., 'The Late Sir Arthur Pearson', in *Headquarters Gazette*, January 1922.
14. Obituary, Cyril Arthur Pearson, *The Wykehamist*, 13 February 1922.
15. From *Idle Thoughts from Darkland*, an anthology of prose and verse, T. M. Miller, Cape Town, 1922.

Chapter 26: St Dunstan's Without Pearson

1. Fraser of Lonsdale, Lord, *My Story of St Dunstan's*, p. 86.
2. 'Lost Hospitals of London: St Dunstan's Hostel'. http://ezitis.myzen.co.uk/stdunstans.html
3. From 1923 until 1953, Sir Neville Pearson served as the Chairman of Newnes Publishing Company.
4. Wooller, Frank C., 'The History of the Blinded Soldiers of St Dunstan's Australia'.
5. Fraser, Lord, *op. cit.*, p. 82. In 1951 Askew was awarded the CBE.
6. 'Lost Hospitals of London: St Dunstan's Hostel', *op. cit.*
7. Castleton, David, *In the Mind's Eye: The Blinded Veterans of St Dunstan's*, p. 137.
8. 'Clock of 1671 to Return', *Saint Dunstan's Annual*, 1935.
9. *St Dunstan's Review*, July 1937.
10. *Ibid.*, January 1938.

11. *Ibid.*, July 1937.
12. *Ibid.*, July 1937.
13. *Ibid.*, July 1937.
14. *Ibid.*, October 1938.

Chapter 27: The Second World War

1. *St Dunstan's Review*, July 1940.
2. Castleton, D., *Blind Man's Vision*, p. 111.
3. Fraser of Lonsdale, Lord, *My Story of St Dunstan's*, pp. 278-85.
4. *St Dunstan's Review*, February 1940.
5. *Ibid.*, April 1940.
6. *Ibid.*, May 1940.
7. *Ibid.*, July 1940.
8. *Ibid.*, July 1940.
9. *Ibid.*, September 1940.
10. *Ibid.*, November 1940.
11. *Ibid.*, December 1940.
12. Fraser of Lonsdale, Lord, *op. cit.*, p. 290.
13. In 1946, Lord Normanby became Chairman of the National Library for the Blind, and its President from 1977.
14. Ansell, Colonel Sir Mike, *Soldier on: An Autobiography*, p. 92.
15. *Ibid.*, p. 92.
16. 'Lost Hospitals of London: St Dunstan's Hostel'. http://ezitis.myzen.co.uk/stdunstans.html
17. Fraser, *op. cit.*, p. 291.
18. Ansell, *op. cit.*, p. 93.
19. Fraser, *op. cit.*, p. 293.
20. Hall, Coryne, *Princesses on the Wards*, Chapter 12, 'The World at War Again'.
21. *St Dunstan's Review*, April 1941. In fact, Melplash Court, Netherbury, West Dorset is near both Beaminster and Bridport.
22. *Ibid.*, April 1941.
23. In October 1914 the British Red Cross Society established the Invalid's Comforts Section whereby medical supplies and foodstuffs could be supplied to sick or wounded prisoners of war. The Section also operated during the Second World War.
24. *St Dunstan's Review*, May 1941.
25. Fraser, *op. cit.*, p. 291.
26. The Braille Institute, Los Angeles, was founded in 1919 by J. Robert Atkinson, a cowboy from Montana who had been accidentally blinded by a gunshot. Shirley died in September 2013. She was survived by her son, Wyndham Bradford Gary.
27. Fraser, *op. cit.*, p. 293.
28. *Ibid.*, p. 294.
29. Ansell, *op. cit.*, p. 100.
30. Information kindly supplied by St Dunstan's Auckland Museum, Blind Foundation, New Zealand.
31. Castleton, D., *op. cit.*, p. 133.
32. Information kindly supplied by NZDF Personnel Archives and Medals.
33. Information kindly supplied by Blind Foundation, New Zealand.
34. Castleton, *op. cit.*, p. 91.
35. Fraser of Lonsdale, Lord, *My Story of St Dunstan's*, p. 313.

Chapter 28: The Great Work Continues

1. Castleton, D., *Blind Man's Vision*, p. 107.
2. *Ibid.*, p. 108.

3. Said Fraser, 'It may surprise your Lordships to know that this year no fewer than twenty men entered St Dunstan's now wholly blind as the delayed result of mustard gas affecting their eyes long ago.' *St Dunstan's Review*, December 1958.
4. *Ibid.*, December 1958.
5. Ansell, Colonel Sir Mike, *Soldier on: An Autobiography*, p. 105.
6. *Ibid.*, p. 154.
7. *St Dunstan's Review*, August 1958.
8. Information kindly supplied by Patricia Dean.
9. *St Dunstan's Review*, June 1957.
10. *Ibid.*, August 1958.
11. Ian Fraser's father William Percy Fraser was a South African businessman. He had emigrated to that country in the 1870s.
12. *St Dunstan's Review*, February 1956.
13. Hall, Coryne, *Princesses on the Wards*, p. 52.
14. *St Dunstan's Review*, September 1958.
15. *Ibid.*, December 1958.

Chapter 29: Post-War Timeline of Events

1. Castleton, *op. cit.*, p. 145.
2. *St Dunstan's Review*, June 1957.
3. *Ibid.*, June 1957.
4. Wooller, Frank C., 'The History of the Blinded Soldiers of St Dunstan's Australia'.
5. Information kindly supplied by Patricia Dean.
6. Hall, *op. cit.*, p. 51.
7. Castleton, *op. cit.*, p. 163.

Epilogue

1. *The Times*, 12 December 1921.
2. Pearson, Sir Arthur, *Victory Over Blindness*, viii.
3. *Ibid.*, p. 316.
4. *The Times*, 10 December 1921.
5. *The Concise Oxford English Dictionary*.
6. Parker, Edward Hazan, 'Funeral Ode on James A. Garfield'.

Bibliography

Adams, James G., *Growing Up through the Great War* (Bitterne Books Hull, UK, 2004)

Ansell, Colonel Sir Mike, *Soldier on: An Autobiography* (Peter Davies, London, 1973)

Baden-Powell, Robert S. S., *Scouting for Boys* (Oxford University Press, 2004)

Berkeley, Reginald, *The History of the Rifle Brigade in the War of 1914–1918* (The Rifle Brigade Club Ltd, London, 1927)

British Journal of Ophthalmology, Vol. 12, 1918

Burns, Ross (editor), *The World War I Album* (Warfare, London 1991)

Carr, Carolyn Jane, 'A Most Creditable Production': *Chronicles of the NZEF* (New Zealand Expeditionary Force), 1916-1919: Their Publication and Utility for Historical Research': A thesis presented in partial fulfilment of the requirements for the Degree of Master of Philosophy in Defence and Strategic Studies at Massey University, Palmerston North New Zealand (2011)

Castleton, David, *Blind Man's Vision* (London: St Dunstan's, 1990)

Catran, Ken, and Penny Hansen, *Pioneering A Vision: A History of the Royal New Zealand Foundation for the Blind.* (RNZFB, Auckland, 1992)

Collins, Theresa M., *Otto Kahn* (University of North Carolina Press Chapel Hill, NC, USA, 2002)

Concise Oxford Dictionary (BCA, London, 1996)

Congreve, B., *Armageddon Road* (William Kimber, London, 1983)

Cooper, Gladys, *Gladys Cooper* (Hutchinson and Co., London, 1931)

Dark, S., *The Life of Sir Arthur Pearson* (Hodder & Stoughton, London, 1922)

Darwin, Charles, *On The Origin of Species* (Mentor Books, New York, 1958)

Everett, Percy W., *The First Ten Years* (The East Anglian Daily Times, Ipswich, 1948)

Foli, Professor P. R. S., *Pearson's Dream Book* (C. Arthur Pearson Ltd, London, 1902)

Foli, Professor P. R. S., *Pearson's Fortune-teller* (C. Arthur Pearson Ltd, London, 1902)

Foli, Professor P. R. S., *Fortune Telling by Cards* (C. Arthur Pearson Ltd, London, 1902)

Foli, Professor P. R. S., *Handwriting as an Index to Character* (C. Arthur Pearson Ltd, London, 1902)

Fraser of Lonsdale, Lord, *My Story of St Dunstan's* (George G. Harrap & Co. Ltd, London, 1961)

Fraser of Lonsdale, Lord, *Whereas I was Blind* (Hodder & Stoughton, London, 1942)

Fry, C. B., *Life Worth Living* (Eyre & Spottiswoode, London, 1939)

Gelder, Michael, Paul Harrison and Philip Cowen, *Shorter Oxford Textbook of Psychiatry* (Oxford University Press, 2006)

Goodchild, George (editor), *The Blinded Soldiers and Sailors Gift Book* (Jarrold & Sons, London, 1921)

Gotto, Basil, *Memoir* (unpublished).

Hall, Coryne, *Princesses on the Wards* (The History Press, 2014)

Hall, (Joseph) Rex, *The World is Mine* (Inkata Press, Melbourne, 1979)

Heasman, Robert, *Who was Cyril Arthur Pearson?* (Pearson's Holiday Fund, South Croydon, Surrey, 2000)

Herie, Euclid, *Journey to Independence* (The Dundurn Group, Toronto, 2005)

Keller, Helen Adams, *The Story of My Life* (Doubleday, Page & Co., New York, 1903)

King, Richard, *With Silent Friends* (John Lane, The Bodley Head, London. 1917)

Laffin, J. A., *A Western Front Companion* (Alan Sutton Publishing, Stroud, 1994)

Lawson, Sir Arnold, *War Blindness at St Dunstan's* (Henry Frowde, London, 1922)

Light in Darkness: A Brief History of the Jubilee Institute for the Blind: A Record of Great Achievements (Jubilee Institute for the Blind, Auckland, New Zealand, 1928)

Macdonald, Andrew, *On My Way to the Somme: New Zealanders and the Bloody Offensive of 1916* (HarperCollins, Auckland, 2005)

Menzies, Gavin, *1421: The Year China Discovered the World* (Bantam Press, London, 2002)

McIlwain, J., *The Hospital of St Cross* (Pitkin Pictorials, Andover, UK, 1993)

McIntosh, G. C., *The Piri Reis Map of 1513* (University of Georgia Press, Athens, Georgia, USA, 2000)

'Minutes of Blinded Soldiers & Sailors Care' Committee, 29 January 1915 to 12 December 1921.

Ormond, Arthur W., 'A Report on the Ophthalmic Work carried out at the 2nd London General Hospital', St Mark's College, Chelsea, 1914–1919 (HMSO, London, 13 January 1920)

Parker, Eric, *Hesketh Prichard* (T. Fisher Unwin, London, 1924)

Pearson, Sir Arthur, 'My Early Days with Titbits', courtesy of Blind Veterans UK

Pearson, Sir Arthur, 'St Dunstans: The Story of the Blinded Soldiers of the British Army', courtesy of Blind Veterans UK

Pearson, Sir Arthur, *Victory Over Blindness* (Hodder & Stoughton, London, 1919)

Prichard, Hesketh V. H., *Sniping in France* (Hutchinson & Co. London, 1922)

Prichard, Hesketh V. H., *Through the Heart of Patagonia* (William Heinemann, London, 1902)

Saint Dunstan's Annual (S.C.S., Gower Street, London, 1935)

St Dunstan's: A Story of Accomplishment.

St Dunstan's Review: For Men and Women Blinded on War Service (St Dunstan's)

Transactions of the American Ophthalmological Society, XVIII, 1920.

Upton, Chris, *Living Back-to-Back* (The Cromwell Press, Trowbridge, 2005)

Wallechinsky, D., *The Complete Book of the Olympics* (Aurum Press, London, 1996)

War Diary of the 8th Rifle Brigade, The Royal Green Jackets' Museum, Winchester.

Watson, Frank L. (edited by C. B. Purdom), *Memoirs & Diaries: A Territorial in the Salient* (First published in *Everyman at War*) (Knopf Publishing Group, New York, 1930)

Westlake, Roy, *Kitchener's Army* (The Nutshell Publishing Co. Ltd, Tunbridge Wells, 1989)

Winter, J. M., *The Experience of World War I* (Grange Books, London, 1988)

Wooller, Frank C., 'The History of the Blinded Soldiers of St Dunstan's Australia'

By the same author

By Swords Divided: Corfe Castle in the Civil War. Halsgrove, 2003.

Dunshay: Reflections on a Dorset Manor House. Halsgrove, 2004.

Sir Francis Drake: Behind the Pirate's Mask. Halsgrove, 2004.

Thomas Hardy: Christmas Carollings. Halsgrove, 2005.

Enid Blyton and her Enchantment with Dorset. Halsgrove, 2005.

Agatha Christie: The Finished Portrait. Tempus, 2007.

Tyneham: A Tribute. Halsgrove, 2007.

Mugabe: Teacher, Revolutionary, Tyrant. The History Press, 2008.

T. E. Lawrence: The Enigma Explained. The History Press, 2008.

The Story of George Loveless and the Tolpuddle Martyrs. Halsgrove, 2008.

Father of the Blind: A Portrait of Sir Arthur Pearson. The History Press, 2009.

Agatha Christie: The Finished Portrait. Tempus, 2006.

Agatha Christie: The Pitkin Guide. Pitkin Publishing, 2009.

Jane Austen: An Unrequited Love. The History Press, 2009.

Arthur Conan Doyle: The Man behind Sherlock Holmes. The History Press, 2009.

HMS Hood: Pride of the Royal Navy. The History Press, 2009.

Purbeck Personalities. Halsgrove, 2009.

Bournemouth's Founders and Famous Visitors. The History Press, 2010.

Jane Austen: An Unrequited Love. The History Press, 2009.

Thomas Hardy: Behind the Mask. The History Press, 2011.

Hitler: Dictator or Puppet. Pen & Sword Books, 2011.
A Brummie Boy goes to War. Halsgrove, 2011.*
Winston Churchill: Portrait of an Unquiet Mind. Pen & Sword Books, 2012.
Charles Darwin: Destroyer of Myths. Pen & Sword Books, 2013.
Beatrix Potter: Her Inner World. Pen & Sword Books, 2013.
T.E. Lawrence: Tormented Hero. Fonthill, 2014.
Agatha Christie: The Disappearing Novelist. Fonthill, 2014.
Lawrence of Arabia's Clouds Hill. Halsgrove, 2014.

* This is the story of the author's grandfather, soldier and St Dunstaner Thomas Waldin.

Author's website www.andrew-norman.com

Index